Roboto Project
this is why we are the punks
fuck you I am free
— *Bret Strawn*

Building a Better Robot

10 Years of the Mr. Roboto Project

Text by Andy Mulkerin

Created by Andy Mulkerin, Mike Q. Roth and Missy Wright
with Dan Bidwa and Arthur Daniel Allen

This book is dedicated to the kids. Fuck the kids.

Photo on p. i by Charissa Hamilton-Gribenas
Photo on p. ii and iii by Tanner Douglass

The haikus that appear on p. i and p. 114 were originally submitted for a haiku competition held during ADD Fest 6 to commemorate the first four years of the Mr. Roboto Project.

First Edition, copyright © 2011 University of Roboto Press
All photographs © 2011 the individual artists.
All essays © 2011 the individual authors.
All Rights Reserved. No part of this publication may be reproduced in any form without written permission.

ISBN: 978-0-615-55977-3

Published by University of Roboto Press
c/o the Mr. Roboto Project
5106 Penn Ave
Pittsburgh, Pa 15224

Designed and typeset by Missy Wright

For info about the Mr. Roboto Project: www.therobotoproject.org
For info about Building a Better Robot: 10 Years of the Mr. Roboto Project: www.therobotoproject.org/book

This project supported in part by a Seed Award from The Sprout Fund.

Table of Contents

Foreword —*Doug Mosurock*	vii
Introduction	1

A History of Roboto

Birth of Roboto	5
Life in Wilkinsburg	7
Roboto II	12
The Multi-Tool	15
Rules of Roboto	19
Roboto's Place in the Scene	25
The Later Years	28
Moving On	30

Perspectives

Growing Up in Roboto: I am now the MAN, I was once the KID(S) —*Eli J. Kasan*	33
From Weirdo to Roboto: Breaking into Your Own Space —*Michael Siciliano*	35
3.15.02: "I Want Everybody Right Here" —*Joel Grimes*	37
"Bahut dhanyavad, Mr. Roboto" —*Adam MacGregor*	39

## Photos and Stories	43
## Show List	169
## Acknowledgements	191
## DVD contents	192

Foreword

It's been my experience that you're only going to find a very small number of people out there who will commit to a cause like it's their job to do so. Being involved with music on a "scene" level, particularly on the axis that the Mr. Roboto Project spun around in the late '90s, when I was its booking coordinator, relied on that small number to make it a possibility at all.

It still does, though the Internet has made things easier. (No more need for dialers, or to salt vending machines, or to run Kinko's scams, though those are still handy.) What goes into organizing a small performance for a touring rock band depends solely on someone's willingness to build something out of nothing, knowing that they will probably lose time and money in the process. Where will it take place? Am I going to conflict with another event that night? What will I do about a PA, mics, monitors, stands, and someone to run it all? How do I promote this show? What local bands can play to ensure that people will come out? What's the best way to break up a fight? Will my efforts work? Who will take care of the money? Who's going to work the door? What happens if nobody shows up?

The people who show up to your event aren't often concerned with these problems. They will be the first ones to let you know if you fucked anything up. They'll smash the mirror in your bathroom. They'll try to get in without coughing up a miserable $5 to make sure a band can get to the next show without you having to worry about how you're going to pay your bills next month. They'll do everything you asked them not to do. (I was guilty of this as well … shamefully eating my fried chicken from nearby B's Deli down in the basement of Roboto #1, so as not to offend the vegans of the manor.)

It's hard to influence people to support a live band they don't know, and even harder when you remove the social lubricant of alcohol and all the revenue running a bar brings in. Booze and bands go hand in hand, one hand often washing the other. At the same time, Pennsylvania is committed to keeping underage people out of bars, and those efforts run at odds with the ability to book live music for the widest audience possible. They say that once you turn 21, you don't really worry about all-ages shows anymore. There may even be a point where you welcome the age barrier. But for the seven years in between when I realized there were punk and indie bands that played in Pittsburgh, and when I could gain access to a bar, I missed a lot of live shows that I really could have benefitted from seeing.

And it's not as easy to alter a Pennsylvania driver's license as it was in the '90s, either. I couldn't will myself a few years older, and so gave my ID to a co-worker at my work-study position at Carnegie Mellon. He brought it back the next day, having fixed it using a damp towel, a steam iron, some Liquid Paper, an X-Acto blade, and a black ballpoint pen. The card was just the tiniest bit warped at the edge, and proudly declared to whoever was holding it that the bearer of this card was indeed 28 years old. This helped in the intervening years, but it didn't roll back the clock to what I missed, like my only chance ever of seeing Peter Jefferies and Alastair Galbraith on the same stage at the Bloomfield Bridge Tavern. I'm still mad about that, knowing that it happened and I couldn't be there. I was just about as upset when I learned the room that hosted all of these vaunted musical acts was about the size of a postage stamp, and stank of fried onions and dead dreams.

The reason I mention all of this was that the Mr. Roboto Project was then, and is now, a symbol of what can be done when you have a small group of people united behind a common cause. Collectively managed, open to people of all ages and walks of life, it was an agent of change in service of the Pittsburgh's music scene. Roboto opened a space to be filled by the bands that were previously playing in basements of student housing. The people who had gone to those events all lent a hand to see it become a reality. It made things a lot easier. It made sure you had a space that, if you took care of it, you could use again. It fixed costs and addressed its flaws and day-to-day issues. It had decent sound, (mostly) working gear, and could accommodate about 200 people shoulder to shoulder. It fostered a community around it, and brought participants in contact with a place they were told by older generations to avoid. It in turn supported the town that allowed it to happen. It gave several generations of new local bands a home to play, and spawned new involvement with a wide variety of students and transplants in Pittsburgh. Many of the people who were involved with Roboto are still living in Pittsburgh today. Some have paired off together and started families there. Some more are seeing the collective through to its third incarnation, as Roboto closes in on 15 years as a real, working thing. Most, if not all, are agents of positive social change.

Every time I'd catch a rock show at a Pittsburgh bar, I couldn't help but notice how much worse everything looked in there with each passing visit. Every time I'd go to Roboto, I noticed something similar, only that things got better each time I'd return, not worse. The stories you're about to read go a long way in support of that mentality, that when you organize with others and get it together, you can make things easier, more inspiring, and all around better for yourselves and others in the world.

—*Doug Mosurock, October 2011*

Introduction

Everyone has a different definition of "punk rock." It began in the 1960s maybe, or the early '70s, or perhaps 1977. It might've begun with the Stooges, or the Sex Pistols, or the Ramones. It might be nihilistic, or socialist, or anarchist, or libertarian. Violent or pacifist. Positive or destructive.

It's probably fair to say that everyone calling themselves "punk" has some sense of disruption, of offending some establishment. There's something naturally subversive about punk rock and punk culture, and that's the only constant.

It's against that backdrop that the Mr. Roboto Project was established in 1999 – as a space run largely by punks, for hosting punk shows, a venue that was meant to circumnavigate the music establishment and maintain itself under the direction of the very people who would be playing and attending the shows there.

The project – and the ten-year run it would enjoy at its original space in Wilkinsburg, Pa., just outside Pittsburgh – would face (and create) plenty of contradictions. How does a subculture that defines itself by its tendency to offend and disrupt run a sustainable business? How does a music venue operate with a no smoking/no drinking policy? How does a rock 'n' roll community establish rules for its own governance? If the punks are in charge, are they no longer punk?

It wasn't a wholly new idea, of course: 924 Gilman has existed in Oakland, Ca., since 1986, and Roboto was based in part on that venue's operational plan. ABC No Rio, opened in 1980 in New York City, was another space that hosted hardcore and punk shows and played a role in inspiring Roboto.

But it was definitely new to Pittsburgh, as, largely, were the principles of co-operative organizing that the venue would be based on. Co-ops existed in Pittsburgh – the East End Food Co-op is just down the street from where Roboto would stand – but were few and far between, and weren't part of the punk scene.

Shows prior to the establishment of Roboto took place in bars like the legendary Electric Banana, and Graffiti, and they happened at the University of Pittsburgh and Carnegie Mellon University for a time. And they happened in basements, especially in Oakland, the neighborhood where the city's largest universities are located. Houses on Chesterfield Street, the Boulevard of the Allies, Oakland Avenue and Neville Street were hot spots for shows, from the '80s all the way until the late '90s and early '00s.

The Pittsburgh scene of the '90s was on the wane when the Mr. Roboto Project was established, but the bands that put the city on the map during that era – Aus-Rotten, Anti-Flag, Submachine – all played at Roboto at one point or another, a testament to the continuity within the scene that spanned bars and basements, pointed politics and drunken nihilism.

That Roboto has lasted as long as it has – the organization reopened at a new space in Pittsburgh's Bloomfield-Garfield arts district in fall 2011 – is something of an anomaly, and perhaps a testament as much to the cooperative character of Pittsburgh's music scene as it is to the organizational prowess of the venue's founders.

In putting this history together, I've talked to many of the founders, board members, venue members and musicians that made Roboto go for its first ten years. I've attempted to gather the stories that show how the venue came to be and came to persist, and the conflicting opinions about what the venue has and hasn't accomplished.

History of Roboto

Birth of Roboto

The seed for the Mr. Roboto Project came in late 1998 when The El Camino Club of Southwestern PA – the goofy punk band Roboto founding members Mike Q. Roth and Eric Meisberger shared – took a trip to Baltimore with Pressgang, a local political punk band. They played at a venue, Black Aggie's, that had been run in a do-it-yourself fashion by local punks. It was a storefront venue under somewhat dubious ownership – but what struck Roth and Meisberger was the fact that it was working.

"That kind of put the bug in our head," Roth recounts. "[If] these kids who didn't seem too organized, in a city that, from my understanding, had worse luck than Pittsburgh with venues, were able to do this thing, why couldn't we make this happen?"

"At that time, the spaces that were doing DIY shows in Pittsburgh were either bars or university spaces – all spaces where someone was able to say, 'Okay, I'm making money off this, until something goes wrong,'" Roth says. He notes the story of when Rancid played at Bellefield Hall, one of several Pitt campus buildings that hosted DIY shows, and someone burned a flag in the building after the show, effectively ending punk shows on campus for a time. "If that had happened at Roboto, not to say it wouldn't have been a problem, but it wouldn't have been the end of the venue."

Roboto founding member Mike Bolam, who played bass in hardcore and metal bands like Crucial Unit and Warzone Womyn, notes that his initial involvement was motivated by a lack of local spaces for the bands he wanted to see. "Prior to Roboto opening, a lot of grind, thrash and hardcore bands ended up skipping Pittsburgh," he notes.

The idea behind opening Roboto, then, was that the space would be sustainable: having a dedicated space would make punk shows a priority, not an afterthought. It would take the pressure off the renters of the houses that were hosting punk shows as well.

In early 1999, the entity that would become Roboto had its first organizing meetings: Roth and Meisberger invited some active members of the DIY punk scene to brainstorm with them on their new idea. Certain parameters were set: the venue would be cooperatively (but not collectively) run, with a membership base that paid in one way or another. It would be as legit and legal as possible. At first, they set out to buy a space outright.

This was also when the yet-unnamed venue was named: originally, it wasn't meant to stay Roboto.

"We bandied about some names – Keystone Collective, something with Iron City in it," Roth says. "Then for whatever reason, I think the 'Mr. Roboto' song was in a commercial at the time or something, and we joked about it and we decided to stick with it for a while."

"Until we get something better ..." Meisberger adds.

Roboto originally operated with a three-person board; after the first few months with Roth serving as sole coordinator, the charter board members were Roth, Deanna Hitchcock, and local promoter Doug Mosurock. Early on, there weren't delineated duties for each board member, though different members took on tasks they were best suited to – publicity, budget work, maintenance. Eventually, specific board positions (treasurer, secretary, facilities manager) were created. In 2001, when Roboto temporarily expanded into a second venue, the board was realigned to consist of five members instead of three. Board positions were held for one-year terms; each board member could run for re-election as many times as desired.

Facilities management was perhaps the dirtiest job to hold on the board. "I definitely had to clean up standing feces in the basement" after a round of plumbing issues, recalls Meisberger, an early facilities board member. But the most complicated and stressful may have been the position of booking board member – the person in charge of interacting with both member-promoters and bands contacting the venue looking for a show.

Unlike more traditional venues, where one person or agency is in charge of booking the space every time there's a show, Roboto allowed members to book their own shows – so there was no central booker whom bands could contact about getting a particular date. For local bands, the solution was often simply for a band member to join Roboto, and book the date her or himself. In order to accommodate date requests from out-of-town bands, though, the booking board member acted as a liaison between a crop of hopeful bands and a swarm of potential promoters.

Joseph Wilk, who held the booking position on the board between 2003 and 2005, recalls that it was a big job. "I could not believe how many e-mail requests from bands, national and local, as well as promoters looking for venue space, we received – hundreds by the week," he says. "So one of my first tasks – and I'm not sure if I should admit this – was to create form e-mails that I could copy and paste to ensure that every single request was replied to and honored in an expedient and informative way."

But it wasn't without its entertaining moments. Wilk goes on: "It was also hard not to laugh at some of the e-mails I got, such as when Dustin Diamond (more popularly known as 'Screech,' from *Saved By the Bell*) sent us a request for a date, along with a $5,000 guarantee."

Life in Wilkinsburg

After the founding principles of the venue were established, and the name Mr. Roboto Project was coined, Eric Meisberger was put to the task of finding a space to hold the project. The first goal was to find an inexpensive building to buy, perhaps with help from the City of Pittsburgh, and rehab it to be a venue. He and Roth remember the first building they considered.

"I made a couple of calls and a city official took us to look at this place – it was technically in Soho, somewhere on Fifth Avenue between Downtown and Oakland," he recalls. "I remember we dressed for the occasion; I wore a shirt and tie. We went undercover – we wanted to seem like someone who could actually buy a building from the city."

"She wasn't much interested in talking with us or answering our questions," Roth notes.

"So we walked in," Meisberger continues, "and the first thing we saw was that it was a two-story building and the second story floor – you could see right through to the roof. It would have taken thousands of dollars to [get the building up to code]."

The Soho building was the only space within the budget of the project; Meisberger and Roth began to keep an eye out for rental availabilities.

At the time that they were searching for a space to house Roboto, others were putting on shows at MOVE Studio on Wood Street in Wilkinsburg, just outside of Pittsburgh's city limits to the east. Wilkinsburg was a town in distress; many of the businesses that had once lined its streets had vacated in the 1990s amidst crime and poverty.

Wilkinsburg also had a history of activity in the local underground music scene: In the late '80s, it was home to the short-lived venue the Sonic Temple, where the first Pittsburgh shows for bands like Nirvana and Fugazi took place. There was an art space and venue around the same time a bit closer to the city limits called the Turmoil Room that had hosted underground shows as well.

MOVE Studio was a dance studio where lessons took place during the day; on some evenings, indie rock shows came together. Local movers and shakers Shawn Brackbill and Rennie Jaffee booked shows for some of the big names of the time, like Rainer Maria.

"It sounded like an echo chamber," Meisberger recalls.

"It was a dance studio, so there was mirrored glass on both sides, so yeah, it sounded like hell," Roth concurs.

MOVE shows brought Roth to Wilkinsburg for the first time since he'd moved to Pittsburgh; he became curious about the neighborhood. "There was plenty of parking, there was a pizza shop right there, a convenience store down the street. So I thought, 'Why not look for something out here?'"

After a few attempts at finding a space in the immediate area of MOVE were foiled in one way or another, Mark Harvey

Smith, director of the Wilkinsburg Chamber of Commerce, began to help with the search.

"I think he understood from the get-go what we were trying to do," Roth explains. "And the first property he took us to was 722 Wood Street." The space had previously held an antique store that Smith says wasn't well-marketed, and therefore wasn't particularly successful.

"Q approaches me with this group of avant garde rockers, punk rockers," Smith recalls. "And that was right up my alley — I had been a big fan of the arts. [The idea of Roboto] wasn't weird or foreign to me — I grew up with punk rock as a child of the '80s."

Smith hooked landlord Ray Como up with the new renters by acting as an agent — he was licensed to practice real estate — but instead of asking for a commission, he asked Como to become a two-year member of the Chamber of Commerce. Smith's inclination was to find businesses that would work for Wilkinsburg, and the arts was one field he saw potential in.

The Chamber was made up of businesses that Smith said represented the old Wilkinsburg — banks and the like. "I thought it had to be a different bunch of businesses" to serve the community in town at the time. (He would later write a book, *Boldly Live Where Others Won't*, about friendly development in transitional communities; his work in Wilkinsburg, including with Roboto, inspired much of the book.)

Roth and Deanna Hitchcock took a look at the space and thought it had potential; Roth recalls that Como told them they could "make it the next Metropol" if they wanted. At the low rate of $300 per month, the Mr. Roboto Project signed a lease to take over the space.

Roboto was open, but not exactly "finished," in time for its first show: on November 12, 1999, the new venue hosted the second annual ADD Fest, an event begun and originally curated by local musician and label owner John Fail. The show featured ten local acts playing ten-minute-long sets; the keys to 722 Wood had been obtained the day before.

"John, Deanna and I went over and cleaned up and got everything prepared for the next day. Taking John home, I ran out of gas for the first and only time in my life, because we'd been running around so much during the day," Roth remembers.

The baptism of the space was relatively successful. Acts included Kitty Pryde + the Shadowcats, HARM, Meisha, El Camino Club of SWPA, Grand Buffet, Land, Viragos, Crucial Unit, Jumbo, and Disturbed Youth. Some of the bands would achieve a certain renown outside of Pittsburgh, others would break up and recalibrate as Pittsburgh favorites, others would go the way of most young bands, becoming minor footnotes to the scene.

"The only crazy thing was, we didn't have any extension cords or anything — so there was an outlet in the middle of the floor and we had one power strip sticking out of that. It ended up getting moshed at various points during the night."

After the first show, Roboto needed some work: the founders sought approval from borough code enforcement, to

Band	Start	End
Kitty Pryde + the Shadowcats	7:00	7:09
HAKM	7:14	7:23
there is no Name.	7:29	7:40 cutoff
Meisha	7:43	7:54
El Camino Club	8:02	8:11
Grand Buffet	8:14	8:24
Pittsburgh Free Improv / Gary Burtz NTU Troup	8:35 / 8:54	8:45 / 9:04
Mistletoe	9:11	9:18
Land	9:25	9:36 cutoff
Viragos	9:44	9:54
Crucial Unit	10:02	10:12
Jumbo / Disturbed Youth	10:19	10:28

keep the space on the level, legally speaking. It wasn't particularly easy. First, they had to convince the code officers that the space — an empty storefront, essentially — was supposed to be a music venue.

"They said, 'Well, as it is, the capacity will only be about 20 people,'" Roth recalls.

"It was like pulling teeth," adds Meisberger. "Every question, we had to put like — 'And if we wanted to have *more* than 20 people here, how would we go about that, sir?'"

The space had a tin ceiling and needed a firewall installed between the first-floor space and the upstairs apartments in order to be up to code. After a period of a few months with few shows while the venue was in limbo, an agreement was reached in which the landlord would install firewalls for a small rent hike.

When Roboto began holding shows regularly, Smith notes, "it turned Wood Street into a totally different atmosphere." A street that had previously had little going on after 5 p.m. now had after-hours life that generally didn't cause problems, aside from noise. "It was one of my greatest sources of pride," Smith says, with regard to Roboto's place in his career with the Chamber of Commerce.

One concern that came up, though: relations with the venue's immediate neighbors. Not long after Roboto opened, residents of the apartments upstairs began lodging occasional complaints about the noise coming from the space. It was a perennial problem; while the venue was operating legally and the board members said they were clear from the start with the venue's landlord that there would be loud noise and that other tenants of the building should be apprised, time after time, new residents of the building said they didn't know what went on downstairs until after they'd moved in.

While Wilkinsburg's noise ordinance only prohibited loud music after 11 p.m., Roboto's board determined early on that shows on weeknights would be over at 10, and weekend shows would end by 10:30. It was a rule that was loosely applied, but on the whole, only rarely did shows go until 11.

The first six months of Roboto's existence alone involved shows by plenty of non-Pittsburgh bands that would go on to modest, if not major, success: Aloha, Karate, Ted Leo, Q and not U, Les Savy Fav, Atom & His Package.

Milemarker's first show at Roboto, on March 1, 2000, coincided unfortunately with the racially motivated shooting rampage of mental patient Ronald Taylor at a McDonald's less than a mile from the venue — an event that surely didn't help the area's reputation as a town recovering from the trend of violence that had been pervasive in the early- to mid-'90s.

"I remember thinking that was really going to harm any chance of Roboto lasting," recalls Corey Lyons, who played in bands like Aus-Rotten and Caustic Christ, and is currently in Kim Phuc. "I really didn't think it was going to last in the first place, and then with that happening — who was going to bring their kids to Wilkinsburg for shows?"

Deanna Hitchcock painting the walls. *Mike O. Roth*

rαndom access

VENUES // DOMO INNOVATO, MR. ROBOTO

Few '80s rock bands managed to stay relevant in the '90s. Styx wasn't one of them — until now. The title of the Jersey prog-rockers' biggest hit has been co-opted by local musician/entrepreneur **Mike Roth**, whose new, all-ages, Wilkinsburg performance space **Mr. Roboto** opened its doors last Friday. In addition to a sizable stage and audience corral, Roth says Mr. Roboto will eventually contain a free library featuring eclectic literature and a hangout space complete with microwave, coffee machine and comfortable seating; all that's needed are generous patrons to donate these items. The idea for the club originated last December, when Roth's band, the **El Camino Club of Southwestern Pennsylvania**, performed at a similar hotspot in Baltimore. "It was one of those things that's always talked about here, but rarely done," he says. Eager to buck the trend, Roth consulted the Chamber of Commerce, who helped him find a space at 722 Wood St. — just down the way from the **Move Studio**. He intends Mr. Roboto to become a cooperative; for a $25 fee, interested parties receive Standard Membership, which enables them to vote for a board of directors and get discounts on performances. An Associate Membership plan costs $10, and shaves a buck off the door price at 12 shows. As for mood, Roth envisions Mr. Roboto as "a really intimate, friendly environment where someone can feel more than just a show-goer — they can actually influence what happens." On Fri., Nov. 19, Mr. Roboto hosts its second show featuring **Oxes**, **All the Quiet**, the **Weather Channel** and **Dogg & Pony**. Call 247-9639 for info. // **LAURI APPLE** >>

In Pittsburgh article about the Mr. Roboto Project. *Reprinted by permission of Steel City Media.*

INTO 2000 ››››› LIVE

R2-DIY

THE MR. ROBOTO PROJECT IS DECORATED IN THE LATEST HI-TECH CHIC. ›››

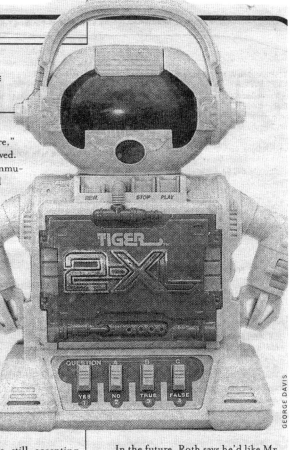

JUST TWO MONTHS AGO, the Mr. Roboto Project — a new cooperative performance venue in Wilkinsburg — hosted its first show: the aptly named "ADD Fest." While a digital alarm clock ticked away, local bands played 10-minute sets for an all-ages crowd. For the club's founder, local musician Mike Roth, it was the beginning of something, um, sort of beautiful.

"A lot of people are happy with the way everything's turned out," he says. "There's still the old apprehension regarding getting out to Wilkinsburg, but attendance is definitely up."

Heading into 2000, the Mr. Roboto Project has already become the favorite all-ages hub for East End punk, indie and hardcore kids to coalesce. Almost 30 people have joined the cooperative as members, including a dozen local bands.

For a $25 fee, interested parties receive Standard Membership, which enables them to vote for the board of directors and get discounts on performances. An Associate Membership plan costs $10, and shaves a buck off the door price at 12 shows each year.

The project has finally captured enough members to hold its first board of directors meeting. "It's not going to be just me in charge anymore," Roth says, somewhat relieved.

The collective's community spirit has spurred several partnerships with nearby businesses. A new tattoo shop located next door has offered artistic services, and a pizza shop down the street has agreed to make more pies on Mr. Roboto concert nights. "Many businesses around us are fairly new," Roth says, "and they're eager because we're bringing people in."

Roth and Co. are still accepting donations for the official Mr. Roboto lounge/zine library. Members have secured a futon, coffee machine and refrigerator, but more lamps and books are needed. In addition to Saturday afternoons, the lounge will soon be open one weeknight — either Tuesday or Thursday.

In the future, Roth says he'd like Mr. Roboto to host a flea market and a punk rock bingo night. "I don't know if it will come to fruition," he says, "but it could be fun." // LAURI APPLE

>> See the winter arts calendar, below, for upcoming shows at the Mr. Roboto Project. 722 Wood St., Wilkinsburg. 247-9639

In Pittsburgh article about the opening of Roboto. *Reprinted by permission of Steel City Media.*

Roboto II

From the time the Mr. Roboto Project moved into 722 Wood, the board was open to the idea of an alternative space. While the Wood Street space worked, it was a bit small (its capacity was 100) and limited in how it could be improved. Something a little larger and more comfortable was always in the back of the members' minds.

In spring of 2001, an opportunity was presented. Roth was approached by a property owner with a space in Wilkinsburg not far from Roboto that would potentially be suited to use as a show space: It was the basement of a boxing gym on an alley off of Wood Street called Stoner Way.

"I don't think it was something we thought about until the owner of the property, Don Scott, stopped by and said 'Looks like you guys have a lot of people here, looks like you could use a bigger space,'" recalls Roth. They weren't sold on the new space at first, but they took a look.

"It was one of those things – the opportunity came up, the risk was low. The rent was cheap. We figured, what's the worst that could happen? If it falls apart, we don't lose much," Roth continues.

The space wasn't exactly built to host shows; it was an empty, subterranean room that needed love, and a stage. In late summer and fall of 2001, a series of volunteer workdays were held to ready the room for shows.

"This was where we parted from our earlier philosophy" of doing everything by the book, Roth says. Based on the lack of concern borough officials had about the Wood Street space, the board didn't see it being all that important to meet every building code – and based on the fact that the room was basically a basement, they knew that it probably wouldn't.

While there were designs on Roboto II eventually replacing the Wood Street space, it began as a supplemental space – one where bigger shows could be booked. But the entire thing ended up being a temporary measure.

In December of 2001, during a Creation Is Crucifixion show, borough fire department and codes officials showed up and weren't impressed with the set-up.

"There were certain things the landlord said he'd do," Roth says, "like open a second door, things like that – that he just didn't do. Surprise."

"I seem to recall, though," Meisberger says, "that the codes people hadn't given us much to work with when we moved into that space, so I think we were pretty surprised when they showed up to shut it down."

"It was surprising, too, because most of our run-ins with the police otherwise involved a little bit of haggling," Roth explains. "They'd come and say there was a noise complaint, and could we turn down, and we'd say 'sure' and they'd leave. But this time, there was a member of the fire department in full gear, the fire chief had a list of specific violations, there was a whole team of [borough] officials there to shut it down."

Interior of the Roboto II space.
Mike O. Roth

The show moved, in progress, back to the original Roboto space – "We carried the PA down Wood Street back to the space," Roth recalls – and that ended Roboto II. Too much would have to be done to bring the space up to code, and the payoff wasn't great enough to put that kind of work into it.

"I think the lead-up to opening Roboto II – when we were doing a lot of work down there, we built the stage, laid carpet – that was one of the periods when I think there was the greatest sense of community and coming together," Roth says. "People who had never picked up a hammer, saying 'Oh, how can I help?'"

"And that was when the shows were great, gas wasn't five dollars a gallon, so bands were touring – we were getting hip-hop acts. That time when we had that space, we had to decide which space would be better. That was a good place to be," says Meisberger.

"It harkens back to what we were thinking when we first got into this, though," he continues. "When we start getting into these handshake agreements – this place, we were definitely paying rent, but there was a lot of give and take with it, and I think once we got back on our footing in the original space, calling the shots the way we wanted to was a little easier."

"And I think that doing big shows just for the sake of doing big shows wasn't where we wanted to be," says Roth. "The show promoters are dealing with booking agents and riders, and [...] getting into fights with [larger local promoters] over who's bringing Converge and dragging us into it ..."

Some at the time suggested that escalating battles between promoters resulted in the shutdown, on codes violations, of both Millvale Industrial Theater and Roboto II. "That sounds like wild speculation," Roth says. "But either way, would we have had these problems if we hadn't gotten into bigger shows? Probably not."

Closing Time

Writer: **JUSTIN HOPPER**
Photographer: **SHAWN BRACKBILL**

The band !!! performs at the now-closed Mr. Roboto Project II.

When the Pittsburgh-bred, San Francisco-based band Creation is Crucifixion hits town Monday (see "Creation Theory" in this issue of *CP*), they'll hope that the show goes a bit differently from their last visit. In December, while mid-way through CIC's opening acts at Wilkinsburg's Mr. Roboto Project II venue, borough fire officers approached the Roboto board members running the show.

"They showed up that night to issue us notice of violation of our fire code," says Mike "Q." Roth, a member of the Mr. Roboto Project governing Board of Directors. "We tried talking to the officials about finishing the show just that night, but they said if they came back, they'd cite us."

Fortunately, when the Mr. Roboto Project, a collectively run independent concert venue, leased their 200-plus capacity space on Stoner Way last summer, they kept the lease for the much smaller venue, around the corner on Wood Street they'd been operating in for two years. For now, the Project's extensive calendar of upcoming shows will all be moved into the Wood Street venue.

"It wasn't really a problem for that show, because it wasn't huge," says Roth. "It was a hassle, though, since — in the middle of the show — we had to move the [sound system], all the equipment, the audience, everything, down the block."

Days after the incident, the Project's board met with Wilkinsburg fire code enforcement officers to discuss what would need to be done in order to bring the venue up to code standards. While some of the tasks, thickening firewalls, expanding exit size, would be easy — after all, the all-volunteer Project had renovated the venue from a disused boxing gym — the venue's basement location and size also made a sprinkler system a requirement.

"And the lowest estimate we could get was around $7,000," says Roth. "Even if we *could* raise that kind of money, is the space worth it? Or should we find someplace better? We were outgrowing [the Wood Street venue], but after trying this, I think maybe we jumped into it too quickly; maybe we weren't as prepared as we could've been."

Roth says that several shows that have been held at Roboto II (the larger, Stoner Way venue) couldn't have fit into the original — and now only — Roboto space. The punk and indie rock shows that make up the bulk of Roboto's schedule are often small enough draws to make Wood Street a viable option, but the growing national reputation of the collective makes a mid-sized venue — a place that can hold shows too big for Roboto, but too small for Club Laga — a goal that the Project will keep in mind. Still, even with the closing of Roboto II, the Project's members may not be too anxious to delve back into the property market.

"We have our monthly meeting this week," says Roth, "and we'll be discussing how we want to proceed from here. It was definitely a good learning experience. Personally, I'm content at the moment to stay where we are but I think it's definitely something we should actively, if not aggressively, pursue."

Pittsburgh City Paper article about Roboto II's closing. *Reprinted by permission of Steel City Media.*

The Multi-Tool

Shortly after Roboto II closed, the Roboto cooperative was offered a chance to expand again, though not into another show space. The storefront at 724 Wood Street, immediately next door to the original Roboto, opened up when the Tribal Skars tattoo parlor moved out. Given the proximity and low rent (the space was also owned by landlord Como), the board made the decision to go ahead and rent out the space. It was to be an incubator space for Roboto-related projects – The Big Idea, the infoshop that had grown during the Roboto II days, moved in, as did Free Ride, a recycled-bike program. Given that more than one project was going on there, the space became known as the Multi-Tool.

Free Ride, in its first iteration, existed briefly in Oakland in the very early 2000s; a local activist named Joy started the operation out of an "occupied house" (a squat) that was soon shut down by the police, leaving the project homeless again.

In 2002, Erok Boerer and Andalusia Knoll, activists and cyclists both, began working on reviving the bike-repair outfit as part of the Wh@t Collective, a group of radicals that met regularly at the time and had largely been behind a May Day 2001 "Reclaim the Streets" party in Downtown Pittsburgh that landed a number of them in jail.

The second coming of Free Ride began at Roboto II, without a lot of planning or, really, know-how. "Joy dropped off his standard ratchet set – it wasn't even metric," Boerer explains. "None of us knew anything about bike mechanics. None of us even knew that 99.99 percent of bikes on the market use metric bolts."

The Roboto II phase of Free Ride wasn't a much greater success than the Oakland phase had been, says Boerer. "Basically, we were in Roboto II, some kids came and stole some bikes and some tools, and then Roboto II closed." Free Ride went dormant until the Roboto cooperative agreed to take over the space at 724 Wood, and offered up room in the new Multi-Tool.

The principle on which Free Ride was founded involved a mostly non-monetary economy: The amount of work one put into the project yielded a certain amount of benefit from the shop. If you needed new handlebars and the shop had a pair of handlebars lying around, you didn't buy them – you donated whatever skill you had to the project, and once you gave a certain amount to Free Ride in the way of work, you got the handlebars you needed.

Organizers viewed it as an indirect form of activism, in more than one sense: For one thing, catering to bicycles encouraged a more environmentally friendly lifestyle, and discouraged car culture. On a deeper level, creating an economy almost completely devoid of currency – and one for which fixed amounts and types of labor were given fixed values not subject to market forces – was itself radical.

Boerer notes that, while (especially early on) many of the Free Ride volunteers were also involved in activist/protest culture, the bike repair project was a different way for activist energy to come out. "We think people should help each other,

Working at Free Ride. *Mike Q. Roth*

we think people shouldn't use as much oil, and we think people should ride bikes more," explains Boerer. "Those were the three things we were really trying to get across, and [Free Ride] was our way of expressing that."

The Big Idea, for its part, grew up in tandem with Roboto. The infoshop began as half bookstore and half record shop – all in a temporary, portable collection that would show up more often than not on a table at Roboto shows.

Books from distributors like AK Press and Microcosm were available alongside pamphlets of radical literature and records ordered from Ebullition, the distributor for many of the punk and hardcore labels that existed (and the entity behind the *HeartattaCk* zine). It was a pairing that made sense: both entities mixed radical politics with loud music and learning.

Just as Roboto was seen as a positive outlet for radical thinking – in its form as a cooperative and as a space for benefit shows for progressive causes like political protest arrestees and the peace and justice organization called the Thomas Merton Center – The Big Idea was a way for leftists, mostly young, some of whom were interested in street-level activism and some of whom weren't, to participate in political activities. Books about reproductive rights were distributed, flyers for marches against corporate globalization and the wars in Afghanistan and Iraq were posted, and vegan cookbooks were sold. Occasionally, the literary events (zine tours, poetry readings) that might have been hosted at Roboto early in its existence were taking place at The Big Idea, next door.

For a time, the Multi-Tool played host to both Free Ride and The Big Idea. It was an idea that made sense in theory – many of the same people were involved in both, the projects were supportive of one another. But in practice it wasn't so simple.

Devon Yates at Free Ride. *Mike O. Roth*

"The Multi-Tool ... was an incubator space," explains Big Idea (and Roboto) founding member Deanna Hitchcock. "Other projects there were getting more established. Free Ride just exploded with bikes, so they needed more space."

Boerer agrees. "Grease and new books don't mix very well, despite our like-mindedness. And we had to store our bikes in the basement, which was awful. I think it was about a year, and then it became painfully clear that the space was not suited [to our needs]. We needed to either take over the whole space or move, and we found a space at Construction Junction," a nearby recycled construction supply non-profit.

On top of the books and bikes, bands had begun to use the basement of the Multi-Tool as a practice space. Over the years, numerous bands – Warzone Womyn, He Taught Me Lies (another band founders Roth and Meisberger were in), Intense Youth! and others – would practice there. One storefront – even spread over two floors – wasn't enough to hold all that.

Free Ride remains in the Construction Junction space to this day. The Big Idea collective members stumbled upon a small storefront in the city's Bloomfield neighborhood – still in the eastern part of the city, but closer to both the universities and the housing that most of the store's patrons were drawn to. The space had previously been home to the office of a state representative; its politics shifted noticeably leftward when the store, now liquidating its record stock to concentrate on book sales, moved in. (In 2011, it moved again, to a space on nearby Liberty Avenue.)

This left the Multi-Tool space to host bands as a practice space exclusively, a setup that continued until late 2005. In December 2005, a water main break on Wood Street directly in front of 724 Wood sent water gushing into the basement

Roboto's basement after the flooding. *Mike Q. Roth.*

space where bands practiced — and kept their gear. Corey Lyons was the first to notice the break.

"I was driving by, headed to my folks' house," Lyons recalls. "I don't even remember why I was going that way, rather than Penn Avenue. I remember looking over as I drove by and saying 'Wait a minute. That doesn't look right.' I pulled over and the sidewalk was caved in, the road was buckling. I called [Mike Bolam] — I didn't even have a cell phone at the time, so I borrowed one from the woman I was with and called him. I felt so helpless."

Bolam remembers getting the call; Warzone Womyn had just moved into another practice space and were practicing there, and he cancelled practice in order to alert other bands and Roboto members, and to go help with the cleanup.

Amps and drums were in about three feet of standing water when band members, Roboto representatives and concerned scene citizens arrived to address the situation. "We had to rent a pump to run water out of the basements" of the Multi-Tool and Roboto, Bolam says, "because the drains were clogged with debris."

"That was the second or third time I thought it was the end of Roboto," Lyons says with a laugh. "I was walking around saying 'This is gonna fuck up the foundation!'"

It was, fortunately, not the end for the venue, or for many of the pieces of equipment, which were salvaged in one way or another. But it was the end of the 724 Wood Street space as a place for bands to practice; it would take months for the landlord to restore the space, and it wasn't worth the wait or trouble for Roboto to stay on a lease there.

Rules of Roboto

While Roboto was always a space devoted to punk rock, it wasn't without regulations: Like the spaces its creators hoped to emulate (especially 924 Gilman), the venue was drug, alcohol, and tobacco-free. It was a double-edged sword – keeping shows clean of substances made the space more comfortable for those underage and kept Roboto from risking underage drinking violations and from the fights and other problems that can plague bar shows. (Wilkinsburg is a dry town, devoid of bars.)

But it also took away the vice that in many cases is part of why people go to rock shows in the first place. The policy became one of the sticking points that would be raised time and again during the existence of the space when critics characterized it as restrictive and uncomfortable.

Meisberger recounts the tension surrounding rules, guidelines and expectations about behavior at Roboto – and the lifestyle associated with it. "I remember the first Lite FM show and Modey Lemon came; Phil talked about radio waves while Paul Quattrone sat there and ate six hamburgers in a row, and I just thought it was hilarious. The idea that there was PC thuggery – I remember somebody said 'I went downstairs to eat my fried chicken because I didn't want to offend anybody.' You've created this notion in your mind that we're all so uptight and holier-than-thou."

"I think part of it was that it was a no-smoking, no-drinking place," he continues. "We simply wanted to make sure it maintained its all-ages status. And [alcohol at shows with minors] was a hassle I don't think we wanted to deal with."

Drummer John Roman, whose numerous bands during the Roboto years included, most notably, Microwaves, played the venue regularly in addition to the bar circuit, and appreciated the lack of drinking at the all-ages venue. "Sometimes, someone may have snuck something in a Mountain Dew bottle, but it was kept well under the radar," he says. "If there were kids showing up with six-packs, that place wouldn't have lasted more than 6 months."

"From the get-go there was a lot of blind-eye stuff," Meisberger says. "You'd have a crusty band and they're all drinking out of their travel mugs. I know they were drinking booze out of those travel mugs. Who cares? You're not being a jerk about it."

Some of Roboto's other rules were more explicitly related to "being a jerk." From the start, the venue's guidelines stated that no racist, sexist, or homophobic speech would be tolerated within the venue. It was, of course, somewhat amorphous: What, precisely, constitutes racist or sexist speech? Do the rules apply simply to the speech at the show itself, or to a band's history, its entire body of work and its album artwork?

It was enough to keep the Supreme Court busy – but the venue's board members made the calls. In many cases, the rules' very existence was enough to keep trouble at bay. But of course there were challenges — some of which didn't even involve Roboto's physical space.

In the early 2000s, the Mr. Roboto Project became known in Pittsburgh for more than just its music venue. The venue's website hosted a online forum, simply called "The Mr. Roboto Project Messageboard," based loosely on punkrock.net and board.crewcial.org, two punk forums based elsewhere.

The message board wasn't really an official edict from the organizers of the collective — Matt Singerman, a Roboto member and, at the time, the venue's webmaster, created the board as an add-on to the site. Growing from a core of 15 or 20 users in its earliest iterations in 2001 and 2002 to hundreds by the middle of the decade, the forum took on a life of its own.

The message board served multiple purposes: On one level, it did allow quick dissemination of information related to Roboto — meeting dates, show notices and the like. But it cut a much wider swath than a Roboto Project-related forum. Show notices for other venues and musician-to-musician talk were just the start of it; current events, politics, and general goofiness took hold and were as much a part of the forum as anything related to Roboto, or even the music scene it was a part of.

At a point, it became clear that it wasn't wise to have a public forum associated with an organization and venue that had certain standards of propriety and respect. While Roboto, the physical space, was relatively easy to keep as a safe space, and it was clear that anyone espousing hateful talk or imagery wasn't welcome and wouldn't be tolerated, it was much more difficult to police a website, and content that was posted that might not represent Roboto's standards would be archived forever on what had become known colloquially as "the Roboto board."

"When I organized an arts and reading event for local transpeople called 'The Tranny Roadshow,' it was subject to public mockery on the associated message board — mockery that was ultimately found and read by the performers themselves," Roboto promoter and onetime board member Joseph Wilk recalls.

In 2006, the split took place: Singerman and Roboto member Jeremy Hedges, who had long been an administrator of the board, migrated it to another server, gave it the URL nevertellmetheodds.org, and divorced the forum from Roboto.

In a more serious matter, in October 2005, a member using the name "Aychbe Wheatstraw" booked a show for a local band called

The flyer for the 1913 Massacre show that was distributed by "Aychbe Wheatstraw."

RACE
Unwanted Poster

Though the directors of local punk venue **Mr. Roboto Project** apologized on Nov. 14 for the racist fliers used by a show promoter, it took a local minister to notice the promotion in the first place.

Jasiri X, minister of the **Wilkinsburg Nation of Islam** mosque, was walking through **Oakland** in late **October** with a few black students when they came across fliers bearing images of black minstrel characters with dark skin and puffy lips.

X had just hosted a meeting on the **University of Pittsburgh** campus with people who attended the **Millions More** 》》12

>>NEWS

>>10

Movement. The march took place Oct. 15 — the same day as the show being advertised at The Mr. Roboto Project, a performance venue and gallery in Wilkinsburg.

The flier said the event was "an evening of audible stimulation featuring sonnets by the world famous minstrels."

"The images were obviously from a time when it was cool to mock black people, which back then was entertainment," says X. "But my biggest problem wasn't the images per se, but the fact that the Roboto Project was a place that operated out of a predominantly black community."

X, Wilkinsburg residents and black Pitt students approached Mr. Roboto's board of directors at a public meeting and demanded an apology. The board complied, saying they were not aware of the flier, since Roboto leaves all promotions to individual show promoters, who must be registered members of the cooperative. It is also Roboto's policy (as their Web site states) to refuse "any performer or promoter a show based on the message or content of the material to be performed (i.e. no racist, sexist or homophobic material)."

According to Roboto board member **Jennifer Briselli**, the group attempted to contact the promoter, who at the time worked under the moniker "**Aychbe Wheatstraw**." His e-mail response, reports Briselli, "included a defense of the fliers as not racist, but 'provocative.'"

The Roboto board tried to hold a meeting between the promoter and activists including X and **Folayemi Agbede**, a black student at Pitt. The promoter, whose phone number indicates he was local and who was registered on their membership list under another fake name, **Joe Hatbob**, would not respond, says Briselli, so his membership was revoked.

The promoter's phone is disconnected and he did not return e-mails requesting comment.

The flier's images were bracketed by text from the **Unabomber Manifesto** written by **Ted Kaczynski**, reading in part: "The leftists will reply that the last thing they want is to make the black man into a copy of the white man; instead, they want to preserve African American culture. But in what does this preservation of African American culture consist? It can hardly consist in anything more than eating black-style food, listening to black-style music, wearing black-style clothing and going to a black-style church or mosque. ... In all ESSENTIAL respects, more leftists of the oversocialized type want to make the black man conform to white, middle-class ideals."

Paradise Gray, an educator and musician in Wilkinsburg, was part of the group that approached Roboto about the fliers. He says the people at Roboto, "to their credit were very receptive and understanding," a sentiment echoed by X and others. Sometimes, Gray adds, progressive white people "are blinded to the fact that racism is alive and well in America and sometimes they take lightly the issues that are sensitive to us."

Still, for Gray, there's a major issue in Wilkinsburg that is still unresolved: "You look around and see no venues for African-American artists anywhere but it's so amazing how the young white kids have this great outlet in a *black* community where we don't have anything."

Pittsburgh City Paper article regarding the controversy. *Reprinted by permission of Steel City Media.*

AN APOLOGY

The Mr. Roboto Project would like to apologize for a flyer that was disseminated in the Oakland area in our name. The flyer (pictured here) was for an event on October 15th at our venue. Although the members of our Board of Directors were unaware of this flyer's existence and did not endorse its creation, it nonetheless was created by a member of our cooperative for promotion of an event at our venue and thus we accept full responsibility. The offensive, insensitive, historically inaccurate and racist imagery used on this flyer is damaging enough on its own, but worsened by the Mr. Roboto Project's presence in a predominantly African-American community. At this time, the promoter responsible for this flyer, who goes by the moniker Aychbe Wheatstraw, has been suspended from promoting any more events at the Mr. Roboto Project. His membership in our cooperative is under review and we reserve the right to revoke his membership should he fail to act accordingly to make amends for his actions (including but not limited to meeting with the Board of Directors and concerned community members, as well as making a formal apology of his own.) The actions of this promoter are a direct violation of our core values, as well as our policy prohibiting performance and promotional materials that include "sexist, racist, homophobic or material that otherwise disrespects or threatens individuals."

As always, the Mr. Roboto Project would like to invite any community members to be actively involved in our cooperative or to bring any concerns regarding our activities to our attention. It is our desire to not just exist within the Wilkinsburg community, but to be an active and positive member of the community. Should you wish to be involved, you can stop by any of our events, attend our monthly meetings (whose dates we try to keep posted in this window), e-mail (info@therobotoproject.org) or call us (412-247-9633).

Signed,
The Mr. Roboto Project Board of Directors
Michael Bolam
Jennifer Briselli
Jim Robinson
Mike Q. Roth
Michael Siciliano

The apology posted by the board of directors.

Follow up article that appeared in *Pittsburgh City Paper* regarding the controversy. *Reprinted by permission of Steel City Media*

The 1913 Massacre. Nothing about the member or the band seemed amiss from the start — plenty of local shows booked at the venue went off without a hitch. But the show would soon put the Mr. Roboto Project at odds with the community that surrounded the venue.

The promoter, whose Roboto membership was filed under a false name, made and posted a flier promoting the October 15 show — one that board member Mike Siciliano told *Pittsburgh City Paper* was different from the one the promoter presented at the venue itself. ("He instead made separate fliers with only the date, time, and names of the bands on them," Siciliano told reporter Brentin Mock.) The offending flier included art based on ads for a 19th-century New Orleans minstrel show, and used text written by the Unabomber, describing "white leftists'" take on "black culture."

Nation of Islam minister Jasiri X happened upon one of the fliers, rife with the imagery of racial sterotyping, and, along with a group of students from the University of Pittsburgh and local African-American activist and musician Paradise Gray, demanded an apology from Roboto. Jasiri X told Pittsburgh City Paper that the aspect of the episode that most troubled him was the fact that Roboto was, as he saw it, a white venue in a black neighborhood — a group of young white people taking advantage of space in a black community without including that community, and now showing insensitivity toward it.

Roboto board members attempted to set up a meeting between Jasiri X and the students and Aychbe Wheatstraw, but were unsuccessful; the promoter's membership was revoked after the board was unable to maintain contact with him on the issue. In e-mail communications with the board and with City Paper, the promoter defended the fliers as "provocative" but not racist, and insisted that he had presented the fliers at the venue ahead of the show and was not reprimanded until the outside community intervened.

Jasiri X and Roboto board members eventually met without the promoter.

"At first it was pretty tense," recalls Jim Robinson, a board member at the time. "And I think the group of concerned folks expected us to be resistant to their recommendations of how to address this issue. "

"Aside from [the suggestion that we revoke] the promoter's membership without giving him a chance to address the issue, we were on the same page about how to amend this issue. We agreed to write a public apology and post it outside Roboto, and take down all the fliers the promoter had wheatpasted in different areas around town."

When Roboto representatives cooperated with the activists and community members who were concerned about the fliers, and expelled the member who was responsible (and not cooperative), the issue passed. But it had brought to the surface some concerns about how the venue was viewed by its surrounding community, and by its membership. While the rules were explicit that racism, sexism, homophobia and other prejudices were unwelcome at the venue, some clearly saw the very intrusion of a primarily white venue in a primarily black community to be out of line. And in a loose cooperative, not every aspect of the venue's public face could be kept under control at all times.

A hardcore scene figure named A.J. – who went by xAJx – who attended and later played and promoted shows at Roboto throughout the decade – says that, while he doesn't feel that one can pinpoint an exact political philosophy for the venue, the culture of Roboto with regard to language changed his behavior in positive ways. "I will say that the space was directly responsible for my cessation of using the word 'faggot.' Despite never having ill feelings toward anyone of a different sexual persuasion, the power of what I thought at the time to be a simple word was never called into question [until I saw it] brought into conversation at Roboto."

The issue of gentrification had reared its head numerous times with regard to Roboto: Wood Street was, before Roboto's arrival and during Roboto's existence, a largely low-rent business district. A convenience store, a Chinese restaurant, a small bread bakery, a salon – the businesses on the blocks surrounding the space at 722 Wood were not high-end retail. Occasionally it was argued, mostly by activists tangentially related to the venue, that a venue like Roboto was the first step toward gentrification in the area – introducing trendy businesses that would raise the rent and drive current tenants away from their businesses and homes.

While the argument was heard, it wasn't one that most of the venue's active members were concerned about in practical terms.

"I think it was after the failure of Roboto II that we had this community group meeting with Roboto, The Big Idea, Free Ride – that's when I think it started to rear up in discussion," Roth says. "A couple people were talking about it, but it was like – we've been here two years, and to be blunt about it, the neighborhood's gotten worse. We lost the pizza shop, there were a couple places that shut down."

"Really," he continues, "the more I'd learn about Wilkinsburg and its government and everything – this is a neighborhood that could use any stability it could get, whether it's a punk rock club or a pizza shop or whatever."

Meisberger agrees: "To me, personally, I felt that bringing that up at that point – are we bringing this up because it's a legitimate concern for the community, or are we bringing this up because we think we should be bringing this up, because we're all forward-thinking, progressive-minded punk rockers? And if that's all it is – we're just patting each other on the back because we know what this word means, and let's make sure we're not it – then is it really that important?"

Jessica Ghilani, who was a board member early in the life of Roboto, adds, "I think that I was more concerned about gentrification as a linear, cause-and-effect relationship then than I am now, or than I was later [during the existence of Roboto on Wood Street], when I knew a little more about Pittsburgh and the way that gentrification works or doesn't work here. It's not quite such a linear process.

"I think that as many suburban parents that heard their kids say 'I'm going to Wilkinsburg' – when Wilkinsburg isn't a place that, from the television news, you'd expect to see a bunch of suburban white kids going – that's interesting, to see that undoing the notion that the city is a dangerous, horrible place. It's interesting to look at that as a long-term result of Roboto as a space, as opposed to being a gentrifier. It's not like there's a Starbucks or a Gap there now, or there will be anytime soon."

When the Wood Street space closed its doors in early 2010, the block hadn't changed a great deal from its state when the venue opened just over ten years prior. A few businesses had opened and few others had closed, but to the casual observer, the neighborhood was largely static. The small scale of Roboto, the limited appeal of most of the shows taking place there, and the general non-commercial nature of the venue and its denizens made gentrification a non-issue in practical terms.

Roboto's Place in the Scene

Small rock shows happened elsewhere in the early 2000s: Millvale Industrial Theater hosted alternative shows of all sorts until its demise in 2002. REA Coffeehouse at Chatham College hosted occasional shows, though those slowed to a trickle as the decade progressed. Quiet Storm cafe hosted some indie bands. Basements in South Oakland persisted but became less prevalent at the time as well.

One thing that set Roboto apart was its not-for-profit nature, and its cooperative economic model. Promoters getting involved with Roboto were almost exclusively people who didn't promote shows for a living – they were folks in bands, and music fans who wanted to book a favorite band, and activists looking to book a benefit show for whatever cause.

When Roboto opened, it was largely seen – at least by its founders – as filling a void that existed in the local scene, not diverting action from existing venues. Most of the punk shows happening at the time were in the basements, and a full-time venue was a welcome addition to take the burden off of those houses.

While it was a punk venue through and through, early on, Roboto hosted more indie rock shows, and eclectic shows featuring multiple genres, but even then, it was more of a venue where bands played before they were big than one where established acts ended up. Bright Eyes played there. Explosions in the Sky played there before Friday Night Lights brought them fame.

In late 2001, local punks-gone-international Anti-Flag filled Roboto for two shows during which they recorded a live album. Both shows sold out; a truck out front served as the control room for the recordings. The band played from the raised stage area – not a common occurrence at the venue, where most bands set up on the floor. (Most bands, of course, didn't pack the venue to capacity, though.)

"I had played in another band that played at Roboto a lot," recalls Anti-Flag's Chris #2, referring to the band Whatever It Takes. "We'd play there, like, every Friday night, and there'd be three people and a lot of pizza. I remember we were talking about doing an [Anti-Flag] live record, and thinking instead of doing it at one of the other venues around town where we played, let's do it for the people who really care about the band, and do it at Roboto. People who enjoy punk rock should know about this place, and some of the people listening to Anti-Flag considered themselves punk rockers but didn't know about this place.

"We did it, and we put these tickets up, and it was like – moms were calling, '*Where* do you want us to go?' I'm sure Roboto got phone calls too. I remember having to deflect all these questions – if you're worried about the area, come to the afternoon show, it'll be OK."

Some people came from far away for the Anti-Flag show: Corey Lyons recalls meeting one man who'd brought his son from Texas to one of the shows as a birthday gift.

"I went over and started talking to him, because he was this dad hanging out outside Roboto – nobody was gonna talk to him, he was just standing there. And he explained that this was all his son wanted, and I thought, this is a pretty cool dad. And he said 'He couldn't have wanted to go to Disneyworld.' And I thought 'Yeah, this sure as hell isn't Disneyworld, buddy.'"

Some of the best attended shows at Roboto, though, were local bills: the March 2002 CD release show for local band Pikadori, which played plenty of shows at Roboto in its day, filled the room (and is described on page 37 by Pikadori guitarist and longtime Roboto member Joel Grimes). Another all-local bill – Teddy Duchamp's Army, Whatever It Takes, Pikadori, Tabula Rasa and Crucial Unit – in the spring of 2002 raised money for the Greater Pittsburgh Women's Shelter and sold the venue out.

Modey Lemon was a local band that was up-and-coming at the time of Roboto's founding, and played shows there regularly in the venue's early years as the band matured and rose in popularity locally and nationally.

"Modey Lemon was pretty apolitical," explains singer-guitarist Phil Boyd, "and I admit that early on we didn't really know if we quite fit anywhere, Roboto included. It became pretty apparent that though there were politics and political ideas being shared, Roboto was also a place for people to have fun. Sometimes the word 'politics' carries a serious tone, but while serious ideas were discussed, people also had a sense of humor and didn't mind letting us get stupid."

David Bernabo played Roboto in the mid-2000s with Boxstep and Vale & Year, bands that didn't necessarily fit the punk/hardcore aesthetic most often applied to the venue, as well as some other short-lived and one-time ensembles. Having played the venue when he was young – and not so close to "punk" ethics or aesthetics – he recalls not being as interested in the politics of the venue as the music and art.

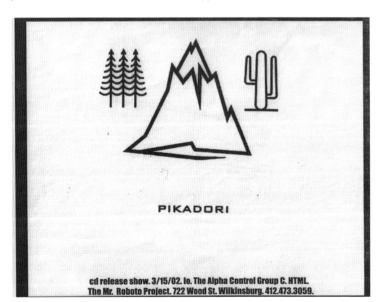

"At the time I was going to Roboto a lot, I was not very interested in politics." he explains. "That came later. The politics did not impact me negatively, though."

He recognizes Roboto as a political entity, however. "Most music venues have no politics," he adds, "or if they do inherently have politics, they are linked to capitalism, and, usually, a floating ethics if the venue is also a bar."

"I felt that depending on the type of show, the political vibe of the room could be very different from the night before," recalls show promoter Dan Rock, who went on to found the Lock and Key Collective (a show promotion organization and label). "So I don't think Roboto had its own politics. It was just a space for people in the community to come and discuss their politics."

In the mid-2000s, several members of the Roboto community, from board members to promoters to show-goers (the author of this book included) were included in a scholarly article by Emory University grad student Stewart Varner called "Youth Claiming Space: The Case of Pittsburgh's Mr. Roboto Project." The article – published as a chapter in the 2007 book *Youth Cultures: Scenes, Subcultures and Tribes* – documented from an anthropological perspective the way Roboto came about and was run.

As the decade progressed, many of the indie rock shows that might've gone to Roboto were moving elsewhere: ModernFormations Gallery and Garfield Artworks, two galleries in the Garfield neighborhood that were roughly the same size as Roboto, began hosting shows. Manny Theiner (once of Millvale Industrial Theater and the Sonic Temple) took over booking, and eventually curating, Garfield Artworks in the mid-2000s. ModernFormations, booked initially by co-founder Devin Russian and later run solely by co-founder Jennifer Quinio Hedges, operated on principles that the owner picked up, in part, from Roboto.

"I saw !!! at Roboto II," Russian, who's since moved to New York City, explains. "The fact that you could see a show like that in Pittsburgh kinda blew my mind. They turned the lights out and only a spotlight held by the singer lit the place."

When ModernFormations began hosting shows in late 2001, Russian says, "I definitely know I was eager to recreate that kind of atmosphere." Many of the bands that played ModernFormations early on were bands that also played Roboto often, a fact that Russian attributes to the fact that Justin Rathell, a friend whose band practiced at ModernFormations, played Roboto often with the band Alpha Control Group C.

In the mid-2000s, ModernFormations would become almost a companion venue to Roboto, with some of the same promoters putting on shows at both venues – louder punk and rock shows at Roboto, and indie rock and acoustic shows at ModernFormations.

xAJx would go on to found a short-lived venue outside of the city, Planet of the Apes, based partly on what he found at Roboto. "It started out as a cooperative but ended up being a one-man show," he explains. He says he was drawn to the venue for reasons he couldn't explain, then found that his own style – as a musician and promoter – was affected a great deal by the way he saw Roboto operating.

He first attended a show at Roboto in spring 2001. "I remember all the details because I was so blown away by basically every aspect of the show," he explains. "I was blown away at the size, the inclusiveness, and the overall sense of community found within the space. It was also nice to be able to breathe without hindrance and to go home without being drenched in alcohol."

The Later Years

In 2006, Brillobox, a bar venue in Bloomfield, opened, and quickly began hosting rock shows for both local and national acts. Gooski's and the Rock Room (once the Warsaw Tavern) in Polish Hill ramped up their show quotients, as did the 31st Street Pub in the Strip District, and Garfield Artworks began having shows at least four or five nights per week; suddenly, there were many more venues for small shows than there had been earlier in the decade.

"Gooski's had always been around, but now Gooski's does the same type of stuff Roboto was doing, on a more regular basis," Roth said in 2010. "And other places have popped up that consistently do shows – Garfield Artworks, ModernFormations, Belvedere's, whatever. We have to say, 'Why are people choosing this venue over Roboto?' And what it ended up coming down to a lot was location."

Other punk shows that might have come to Roboto earlier in the decade were, by the waning years of the decade, taking place at 222 Ormsby, a house venue in the Carrick neighborhood, south of Downtown – a venue booked often by the Lock and Key Collective.

Lock and Key founder Dan Rock explains that, while he never officially broke with Roboto, he found that the venue's reputation amongst a lot of the people who might be interested in his shows prevented the kind of turnout he would've wanted there.

"It seems from day one there was always some kind of anti-Roboto sentiment," he explains, "and people would make up these insane stories about the place – stories about people being kicked out for eating meat, or how cliquey and unwelcoming it was. Eventually the people who took over did get a little cliquey. I just tried doing any particular show at the place that made the most sense at the time."

In the later years of the decade on Wood Street, with so many shows happening at venues that had popped up around town in the mid-'00s, the diversity of the music played at Roboto lagged. But it remained a venue that supported its scene: A certain brand of hardcore – political, often straight-edge, but also concerned with moshing – became the most visible genre at the venue.

xAJx started the band Path to Misery in 2006, and played and promoted plenty of shows in the late 2000s at Roboto. He stepped into a board position as he saw many of the original proponents of the space stepping down from their positions and putting on fewer shows.

"I wanted to run for the board from day one, but never wanted to feel as though I was intruding on someone else's spot," he explains. "When it seemed as though a lot of the 'original members' seemed to lose interest in the spot, I decided to step up – the facilities position was uncontested. It felt good to apply all of the knowledge I gained from fucking up my own spot to a venue that, at the time, seemingly needed it more than ever."

Roboto was still serving the purpose it always had: providing a space for music that didn't have a space elsewhere. But exactly what that music was had changed a bit: Indie rock, pop punk and avant-garde music now had their own venues. Hardcore – with its moshing, spin-kicks and the like, and straight-edge sensibilities – had no other venue. No gallery would allow that kind of dancing, no bar would welcome bands that specifically eschew drinking (and few bands that eschew drinking would want to play a bar).

Moving On

February of 2010 was the last month of the Mr. Roboto Project at 722 Wood St. in Wilkinsburg. The board was working on finding a new space for the venue, and the old space wasn't holding as many shows as it once had. Rather than hemorrhage money, the membership decided to pack it in on Wood and concentrate on finding and opening a new space – perhaps losing the old space would be the kick in the pants the organization needed in order to get the new space off the ground.

A weekend of farewell shows was held; longtime members came to offer their last respects, and some classic "Roboto bands" (He Taught Me Lies, which had effectively disbanded a year before; Allies, the band that rose from the ashes of Pikadori; Warzone Womyn, whose members were all on the board of Roboto at one time or another) played along with some newer regular denizens of the venue.

As is evidenced by the roster of bands that played shows there in the early part of the 2000s then went on to become household names, the venue introduced to Pittsburgh a lot of punk and indie rock talent that might have passed the town up had it not existed. Beyond the acts like Bright Eyes, Ted Leo and Tragedy, there were Kylesa, Coliseum, Municipal Waste, Fucked Up – bands that would end up at bigger venues by 2010, but had nowhere but Roboto to play in, say, 2006.

Roboto didn't introduce the idea that shows could exist outside of a bar atmosphere, but the venue popularized the idea with a generation of showgoers. There had been other non-bar venues – the Sonic Temple in 1989, and Millvale Industrial Theater later on. But Roboto, along with ModernFormations and the short-lived Project 1877, and later Garfield Artworks, was part of an early-2000s trend that made it common for shows in Pittsburgh to happen in a barebones room with a capacity of 100 or 150.

In March 2011, the board of directors announced it had found a new space on Penn Avenue on the border of the Bloomfield and Garfield neighborhoods of Pittsburgh. Bigger than the Wood Street space and outfitted with more comforts – and two separate rooms – the space officially opened in November 2011.

Re-opening in a more saturated venue landscape (albeit in a more convenient location) could be the final proof of Roboto's success. But even before the new space was determined, founder Roth expressed that Roboto could be seen as having done its job. "We want to do our thing and do it well," he says. "And if we're doing that, we're creating this space, and as long as people want that space, we'll continue to exist. And if nobody wants that space anymore, then we cease to exist – and we've done our duty."

Growing Up in Roboto:
I am now the MAN, I was once the KID(S)

I first heard about the Roboto Project at whatever Vans Warped Tour that was around the time of ADD Fest 2. I had received a flyer from the always-hilarious Greg Solomich and I can remember his words plainly to this day: "We have a venue!" I was excited but I decided to skip seeing Good Clean Fun. (I still count this as a good move on my part.)

Growing up in the 'burbs I had limited access to what was what I would clearly define as "Punk™," "DIY" or "Indie" now. Back then it was renting a VFW hall and using whomever's PA system to put on a show; that usually involved the shittiest bands all trying to out-do each other in terms of attendance. It was vaguely ironic that these kind of shows were a strange meeting of the minds in terms of having lots of different genres and people represented, largely due to the fact that high school kids weren't discerning about checking out what seemed to be the only event worth attending besides a Del-Greco pool party.

But I digress; they weren't really that diverse and there wasn't a real sense of community. I wanted the kind of experience I had only read about in the liner notes of a Rhino Records CD punk compilation. (Although I didn't really view Eddie & The Hot Rods or "Everybody's Happy Nowadays" as Punk. 'Cause I was dumb.) I used to read Hoss' Show List and daydream in class about what those bands would actually sound like. It was a real motivating factor in wanting to seek out live music, but at 16 your options are limited.

I had the chance to first play Roboto when I was 16. A few months before our show, there was a gruesome murder at the McDonald's near Roboto. My Dad was very uneasy about me playing in the area & insisted on driving me to the show. We showed up, played shittily (if memory serves) to a dozen punks & with all sincerity felt a great sense of community despite the slim turnout. Practically everyone in the audience was in a band – truthfully, probably 6 of them were in bands playing that night. It was such a great time in my life to get the sounds I had in my head out to someone other than my band mates or my unfortunate parents whose garage was once our fortress of solitude.

When my Dad picked me up, he asked about the turn out and when I told him he said he was relieved that I wouldn't be playing there again. He had misunderstood me, and I continued to play Roboto for the next 10 years or so of my life. Like most people, I think I took the space for granted. In absentia I realized the sentiment that Greg was trying to convey over a decade ago: that I felt at home, met many like-minded people, even my fiancé, at a venue that was more or less mine. I was free to play my guitar out of tune, I was free to mosh like an idiot, I was free to sit in my car and listen to Belle & Sebastian instead of watching Prurient if I was so inclined. (Oh man was I ever!)

It seemed like in its glory years it produced some amazing memories for most involved. Everyone has a story about seeing their favorite band before they were your favorite band, playing their best show, playing their shittiest show, meeting some hot girl or guy or just having something to do besides listening to records. 'Cause that's what I would've been doing if I hadn't discovered the space.

Ed Steck told a story once about how he & Hickey came from the suburbs to see The Locust play. He said that people were going ape-shit: moshing and bouncing off the walls and it was the most insane thing that they had ever seen. (Ed loves to say the word "insane." Listen for it sometime, dear reader.)

The story fast-forwarded a few years to where he & Hickey were cleaning up after a show. It was just the two of them and they started reminiscing about how crazy that Locust show was. Ed said they started trying to re-enact it, jumping off of benches, moshing, doing stupid dances etc. He said he got carried away and slipped off of the bench at Roboto and ate shit really hard. "Straight on my back, dude" is how I recall it being told. He said he lay in agony for a while, feeling old. It was really fucking funny.

The heart of Ed's story was that he grew up at Roboto, he had come there with his best friend: since then he & Hickey were still friends, he'd made new ones as well, saw some amazing bands and forged some really fond memories over his course of visiting the space.

He told this during the last Brain Handle show at Roboto and he was clearly upset about the space closing. The story related to the heart of my essay here; lots of people felt at home here, or shared a special memory with someone here and most people miss it like a dead friend. I do.

Without Roboto I know I would have come to find the same ideals & ethos, but they would have come from a longer search and from a more fragmented approach. I always liked that the space was a leveler: older punx that mostly played bars would play there, ska bands from the suburbs would unfortunately play there, and friends would recycle each other & ideas into 1,000 different bands. It made it really easy to learn a lot about yourself and your instrument when everybody needs a drummer or another guitar player. You ended up making friends or enemies fast. With the absence of Roboto, I feel that it puts people who are older (and I don't consider myself old, not at 27) even more out-of-touch with youth culture, which is the exact spawning grounds for punk in the first place.

I don't see many younger kids, or even college kids, forming new bands and playing around town, but how can I expect to when I mostly see shows at bars? I know there are a number of basements and art spaces, but to me Roboto was the ultimate ground zero of youth punk. And when you start hating the KIDS you slowly become the MAN. That's what it was to me when I was 16, I want to see some kid, even if their band is terrible having that same experience that I had at that age. I'm not trying to be obsequious to the space, but I do believe that Punk had the most profound effect on my life and Roboto was a large part of that.

I won't miss the smell of it in summer though.

In Solidarity,
—Eli J. Kasan, September 2010

From Weirdo to Roboto:
Breaking into Your Own Space

Roboto. Weird spot. I was really into it for a long time. My lifetime membership was purchased in 2006 and, well, "until death do us part." As an active member I probably did 20 or so shows from 2001-2007. Sweat, heartache, getting kicked out of bands, etc. I moved away from Pittsburgh in 2008.

From 2005 until 2007 I was a board member. I took over the schedule coordinator position from "Screamo" Joe Wilk. Through some sort of magical act or sleight of hand, I had ceased to be the weirdo from Ohio and suddenly folks like Manny Theiner and weird suburbanite kids would say "You're one of those Robotos." I'd had something of a bad rep from a dumb high school band and never really seemed to gain acceptance or real friendship from anyone involved in music here, ever. Elitism. Egalitarianism. Or just educated punks electing to perform in storefronts rather than nightclubs? Not to sound too much like Brad Pitt in Fight Club, but "yeah, that is something," however vapid or elitist you might find the motivations.

By 2005 or 2006 the space was hitting a bit of a slump. All of a sudden a lot of the first generation of Roboto folks had grown up and lost interest in the space or gotten burnt out on being board members. Younger kids were not showing up anymore to replace the generation of promoters/Roboto members from which I had come. Hardcore was continuing to rage at Roboto, but the space's previous position as crucial nexus between activism, indie rock, hardcore, and other genres of music had shifted. Roboto was a hardcore venue and while hardcore paid some of the bills, it didn't allow the space to grow.

I felt that we were stagnating and being a co-captain of a ship that was slowly sinking and the fact that I never seemed to be "enlightened" enough for most of the founders of the space made me feel as though Roboto's stagnation was my fault. So the venue was failing, younger people were not becoming members and we had a reputation as being jock macho hardcore thugs among arty, hippie types and a reputation as being hippy, arty, commie, queer, leftist, liberal, etc. among conservative G.G. Allin / Anti-Seen types. This story is from before all of that, it's about a time when I was still considered a bit of an Ohio, redneck weirdo college student making crappy student films and unknowingly playing in a screamo band.

Easter Break-In

It's Easter Weekend 2002. I'm 19. I booked a benefit show for the local Independent Media Center that was starting up. Punk benefit, shitty bands, we made like $60 for the IMC. This was #3 in my series of benefit shows that raised no money. It's the thought that counts, or at least I hope thoughts count. All of my activism is mental and, like so many other folks like me, I didn't accomplish anything worth talking about. Everyone privileges actual action just like the Nazis. "Just Do It." Thoughts, apparently, don't mean shit. Oh, yeah, the show.

Slated for my amazing failure of a benefit show were Sadaharu (post-hardcore/screamo popularizers, not innovators), Crowded Tombs (Swarm-worship), and Monster Through It Be (utter crap). I showed up to Roboto around 6:30. No one was there to open the space. 7pm rolled around. A crowd had gathered. All of the bands had arrived. I was nervous. 7:15 shows up and there's no one with a key. Folks are beginning to talk about leaving the show.

Angelo from Sadaharu said, "Hey Mike, I'm a carpenter. I can remove the door and we can just go inside and start the show." After another fifteen minutes of waiting I gave Angelo the nod to begin disassembling the doorframe and so we were officially "breaking in" to Roboto. I thought "Great, I'm a member for 7 months and I'm already breaking into the place."

Chain-smoking with my back turned to the vaguely illegal actions going on behind me, I received complaints from the Tombs guys. They may refuse to play if we do this. At this point someone offers to go and get Dave Trenga's keys. Awesome. Wish we had known that Dave had a set of keys 15 minutes ago. Brain geniuses. The show proceeded without issue and ended promptly at 10:30. We locked up and left.

Only one really bad thing happened and that was the minor crack in the window that was removed from the door. It was a minor crack that left the window structurally sound. According to internet speculation the window was "broken" by those inconsiderate people who did the show rather than "carefully removed by a skilled carpenter and then accidentally cracked upon replacement." So what does it mean exactly to break into a space that is cooperatively owned?

Following the "break-in," I was lectured by an attendee at the next Roboto meeting. This attendee was never, to my knowledge, on the board of directors, and, again, to my knowledge, was never "punk." This struck me as really odd that I was being lectured by her on what should be done when a venue fails to open its doors for a show that was scheduled well in advance. Nothing against her and maybe we shouldn't have had a carpenter remove the door in order to go in and play a show that made some money for the IndyMedia Center. It is, after all, against the law.

Or was it? Technically I was a member of the cooperative that runs the space, so technically an owner was opening up the space in order to have the space fulfill its stated purpose (to allow for performances and events set up by members of the cooperative). This was, after all, "our" space and I was making use of it. The board let me off the hook for breaking and entering. After becoming a board member in 2005, I never had to worry about entering Roboto. In fact, from 2005-2007, I was more concerned with not being there and when I could just leave the space.

— *M. Siciliano, August 2010*

3.15.02:
"I Want Everybody Right Here"

On March 15, 2002, Pikadori – a Pittsburgh band I played in along with Joey Vesely, Jason Kirker, and Jacob Leger – released our first album to a room full of old friends and new faces at the Mr. Roboto Project. We were fortunate to share that bill with other locals Io, The Alpha Control Group C, and He Taught Me Lies, bands that filled us with inspiration, and – not so coincidentally – were filled with our friends.

As is often the case with intense nights in our lives, my memories of our release show at Roboto are – to be honest – rather hazy. Some eight years later, I can't recount any specific conversations that were had, speeches that were made, or funny incidents that occurred. I can't even tell you what songs were played, how many strings were broken, or how many times the microphone stands were knocked over. It's all become one blur of sound and sweat, faded into the sweet glow you get when you think about a dreamlike moment when so many of your favorite people were all gathered in one place, doing one thing, willingly and with great dedication.

There are a few things I do recall. I have a very clear recollection of singing along to all of the opening bands, despite promising myself to refrain from doing so in order to save some scrap of my voice for our set. I recall feeling the floor buckle and bend several times under the collective weight of so many people in that one single room, bodies pressed together in an engine of pumping fists and stomping feet. I certainly remember roses being showered upon Pikadori at the highpoint of a song, as had become the tradition at Roboto during momentous shows. Later, I would even grab some trampled petals from the floor and pack them away in my guitar case, a soft reminder of how sometimes the crowd is not so faceless, anonymous, disconnected. Sometimes, the crowd is people whom you love, and who love you, and who rain flowers upon you accordingly.

But what I always come back to most about this show was what a watershed moment it felt like in the life of our musical and activist community. I know how hyperbolic and dramatic that sounds, but that night several other people commented on the almost palpable sensation in the air, as though something we had long talked about in merely theoretical and subjective terms had, somehow, suddenly actualized itself in the form of this building, filled with young living beings, their ideas and dreams, and a tremendous sound to hold them all together. Right then, it was as if we were simultaneously realizing that within Roboto, not only had something important happened, but it was – in fact – happening more than ever.

After all, how many years had we, "the kids," sat in basements and garages, the living rooms of communal houses, "the wall" in Oakland – which was, before the internet explosion, where any and all info was exchanged – and talked about a place to call our own? A home for music, art, information, and activism that would not know the limitations of age-barriers and that would be a true reflection of those who participated in it? How long had we dreamed of not needing to convince someone of our intentions or talents, but simply having a space to share them? And when Roboto came into existence, how many of us thought it would become the epicenter of a rabid new energy, the seed of countless friendships, a place that people would talk about and flock to from all over the city, region, and country?

Yet somehow, on March 15, 2002, two and a half years into the existence of Roboto, there we were, the venue filled to capacity with people of all ages who had come not to see a wildly popular national or international act, but instead to celebrate the energy of music created by their friends and neighbors, in a space they themselves operated and gave identity to, on a night where everyone knew the words, as they had supported these bands many times before at Roboto, local labels like Hope Records and Hardtravelin' had released their music, and local record stores and college radio stations were actively promoting such releases. In essence, there was a pulse, and that night it felt like we knew we were at the heart of it within the walls of Roboto: where the engine was, where the energy came from, where the idea actualized. So, when during one of our songs Joey belted out the lyric "I want everybody right here," and I saw the swell of people who were gathered around the microphone screaming that line in unison with him, it was as though I knew then and there that Roboto had truly become our home, everyone had made it in safe and sound from their individual storms, dinner was served in song, friends had become family, and yes – "here," it was indeed "right."

Thank you, Roboto.

— Joel Grimes, September 2010

"Bahut dhanyavad, Mr. Roboto"

If radically politicized, technical grindcore was my escape hatch, then the Mr. Roboto Project was the cradle at the end of the wild chute-ride that followed.

My 25th year found me feeling trapped and frustrated in the suburbs, working a day job as a city reporter in Latrobe, Pa., and trying to figure out whether playing original music in bands really should be part of my plan anymore. I had made the mistake of believing the wrong "advisors," who told me that music certainly wasn't "practical," nor would it get me further in whatever it was that was shaping up to be my career.

As it stood, my long-running band Crank Radio had split up, and most of the venues like Latrobe's Illusions, the Derry Theater, and the Teatro Café in Greensburg where we'd played regularly over our lifespan had shut down or changed formats to accommodate the vagaries of the club crowd. So, I'd resigned to an immediate fate of covering school board meeting after city council meeting, punctuated by – in the interest of full disclosure – the occasional bar gig on the cover-band circuit with Disco Bitch and the Funk Machine, a nine-piece booze-charged trainwreck of a '70s novelty act. (Ironically enough, that would be the last time I ever actually earned money playing music!) These early months into 1999 were a stagnant time when all the possibilities seemed exhausted; all the cool places were closed, all of the interesting people were in the process of burning out or moving away.

When Nathan from (said "radically politicized, technical grindcore" band) Creation is Crucifixion dropped me an e-mail that March asking me to join what was then my favorite band for a forthcoming U.S. summer tour, preceded by several area gigs (one of the first of which was at the Roboto Project), it forced me to put music back on the front burner in what looked like a last chance at doing anything cool – and to reorganize my life to make it all possible. It was not without consternation that I committed to the gig, and planned to put in my notice at work, effectively abandoning that "safe and practical" mode of living that had carried me through a by-the-numbers existence thus far. What followed was a whirlwind year of two U.S. tours and a monthlong European jaunt that saw us playing clubs, squats and youth centers across 10 countries.

It was an experience that planted early seeds for a keen interest in travel and my subsequent study for a career in international development work. I think that those same old "advisors" would have scoffed, calling it all frivolous risk. This decision to "chuck it all" and just go was a pivotal moment that I go back to time and again even over a decade later. I have Nathan to thank for that, and the Mr. Roboto Project to provide a fertile reality on the other side of that leap of faith.

Outside of xeroxing fliers and duping demo tapes for sale at local gigs, the DIY spirit was until now an alien concept for me. In the Westmoreland County 'burbs, we had an active scene of young folks who went to shows and hung out at the same coffeeshops and bars, but no cohesive, purpose-driven "movement" with a shared politic, general aesthetic, or "way of doing things" anything like what existed at the Mr. Roboto Project.

I remember the excitement I felt at the novelty of such a venue and collective behind it – the sense that not only was it possible to set up your own gig — or tour, even — but that many of the bands I'd been fans of had been doing it that way for years. In that sense, Roboto represented an undiscovered cache of possibilities to me – what young people are capable of putting together as an alternative to the prevailing ways of doing things.

What's more, Roboto put Pittsburgh on the map nationally. When CIC played similar places like the Creepy Crawl in St. Louis, Speak in Tongues in Cleveland, or 924 Gilman and the PCH out west, it was always with pride that I could tell other kids that yes, Pittsburgh had a place like this too. And when my old friend Jeff Gretz and I launched Conelrad in 2001, Roboto provided an ideal incubator for our experiments. (Our first gig was opening for Arab On Radar – thanks to David Duncil for taking a chance on us!)

And it didn't stop at just music. I saw others politicizing their creative work, collaborating with artists in other disciplines, or creating efforts at community outreach like Free Ride and the Multi-Tool: nothing was off the table and no means of setting an idea in motion was too impractical. In some cases, these DIY baby-steps led to full-fledged ventures themselves – Bike Pittsburgh and DeepLocal (whose CEO is Nathan Martin, once of Creation is Crucifixion) come to mind. These were the inspirations and values that I took away from Roboto and the creative community of friends that gathered around it.

It's funny, on reflection, how many times I had heard from my elders and authorities that punk rock couldn't teach me anything. It's probably taught me through experience most of what I know about adaptability, planning and organizing – and what truly makes a cooperative community.

— *Adam MacGregor, March 2011*

Photos and Stories

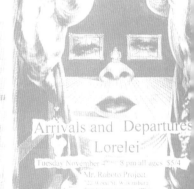

The stories and memories interspersed with these photos were gathered from Roboto members and musicians who played the venue; the majority recall their most memorable Roboto moments.

Kitty Pryde + the Shadowcats, the first band to play Roboto. *Mike Q. Roth*

El Camino Club of Southwestern Pennsylvania. *Deanna Hitchcock*

Grand Buffet. *Deanna Hitchcock*

New Terror Class. *Missy Wright*

Convocation Of ... *Shawn Brackbill*

Convocation Of ... *Shawn Brackbill*

Steevo Cummings, Deanna Hitchcock and Mike Q. Roth.
Photographer unknown.

"I remember there were a ton of different styles of shows at Roboto the first few years. I feel like a bunch of us went to almost every show regardless of what acts were playing. I think on one hand everyone was trying to be open to new and different things and on the other hand a lot of us feared the space would go under if the shows weren't well attended."
—*Ian Ryan (Crucial Unit, Suburban Death Machine, Abort 'Em All Productions and former member of Roboto board of directors)*

DisturbedCaminoLandUnit.
Deanna Hitchcock

Deanna Hitchcock and John Fail, at the Robot vs. Cockroach themed Y2K New Year's Eve party.
Mike Q. Roth

Ian Ryan and Mike Q. Roth, as DisturbedCaminoLandUnit plays. *Deanna Hitchcock*

Mike Bolam, Eric Meisberger, and Ian Ryan at the art opening for the first art show. *Deanna Hitchcock*

Sam Wheeler at the opening for the first art show at The Roboto Project. *Deanna Hitchcock*

Video installation, part of an art show at the space. *Deanna Hitchcock*

"I found Roboto at a formative period in my life; I think we all did. Roboto was instrumental in the development of my love for Pittsburgh, and the carefully upheld attitudes of respect, politeness, and freedom (as I experienced them) helped shape my perspective on taking my own path — one not fettered by the mainstream or by any one subculture."
—*Shahrzad Samadzadeh*

Milemarker. *Shawn Brackbill*

Milemarker. *Shawn Brackbill*

"I met the amazing Joseph Wilk!!!!! My best experience watching a show there was the sound collage he did in honor of his bird who died. It was beautiful and imaginative and fantastical, just like him. I did once get in a lil verbal tiff with the guys from Drugdealer who I actually love over the fact that my band had a song about single motherhood. Nuanced conversation, though, and good."
—*Katy Otto (Trophy Wife, Bald Rapunzel, Del Cielo, Exotic Fever Records)*

The French Kicks. *John Herrington*

Taking Pictures. *John Herrington*

"Summer 2002 was the first show I ever played at Roboto — Hypatia, Robot Attack!, Donna and Carly, and Wolves. It's also the first time I met Carly. Now, almost 10 years later and through the tight-knit community we call the DIY punk scene, Carly and I are playing in the same band and are engaged! We love playing Roboto over any venue in Pittsburgh and we appreciate the fact that it's all-ages and substance-free!"
— *Tom Patterson (Robot Attack!, Slingshot Dakota)*

Disturbed Youth at ADD Fest 2. *Mike Q. Roth*

Discount. *Shawn Brackbill*

53rd State. *John Herrington*

Victory At Sea. *John Herrington*

"I also will never forget the Blood Brothers show where we (everyone standing on the bench) heckled the band during the entire set. ("USA USA USA!" and after a cover of "Under Pressure," "Play Vanilla Ice again!") Sometimes people were jerks at Roboto and it ruled."
— *Jen Briselli (former member of the Roboto board of directors)*

The Great Eastern. *John Herrington*

Les Savy Fav. *Shawn Brackbill*

"I realize that anyone who wasn't there might not find this amusing but I feel it needs to be documented. At one of the ADD Fests there was a performance featuring some combination of members of Grand Buffet and Modey lemon playing a cover of "Down" by 311. There was something magical about them unapologetically playing this decidedly un-punk cover. It's really hard to convey in words the charisma, energy and conviction that was put into this cover. By the end of the song everyone was nodding along and loving every second of it."
—Ian Ryan

Q and Not U. *Shawn Brackbill*

Kill Sadie. *Shawn Brackbill*

"I have so many amazing memories and great shows from Roboto, it's hard to narrow them down—playing Io's first show with Q and Not U on their first tour and falling in love with that band, seeing awesome bands like Yaphet Kotto and Engine Down multiple times in such an intimate setting, being at totally sold out shows like the Locust and Cave In and feeling the walls pulsing with energy ... the RAMBO show with Memento Mori and Steel Curtain at Roboto 2 where it was a Steelers-versus-cops theme, the mosh pit lining up to wall of death each other according to costume and dressing up as vikings with JD ..."
—*Brian Watson (Io)*

Gunspiking. *Shawn Brackbill*

"No Time Left played a criminally underattended show, but about 10 kids from Buffalo drove down to fill the show out a bit. During No Time Left's last song, the singer blew out his knee from jumping around too much, and gave the mic to some kid in the crowd, who finished singing it. In my mind, this completely embodied the DIY and cooperative/community nature of Roboto and shows there."
—*Brian Gruetze (former member of the Roboto board of directors)*

Anti-Product. *Mike Q. Roth*

"My favorite Roboto shows were only partly about the music. The music was important, of course ... friends piled on top of friends to scream lyrics into an out-turned microphone, heads bobbing in unison, circle pits, Gunspiking, Io, World B, Pikadori. But at my favorite shows, what happened after the place closed was just as essential. The bike rides, the french fries and iced tea in near-fatal quantities. A city pool, quiet and dark, with uninvited visitors taking a dip. The sun rising the next morning on a sign or billboard newly adorned with wheatpaste or paint. Some band—from Arkansas, or D.C., or Finland—crashing at our place for the night and waking up to pancake breakfast. A good show at Roboto was a key ingredient in the fuel we burned while we worked hard to make good things thrive in the iron city ... projects, art, gardens, babies, friendships. A good show at Roboto not only conjured up that powerful, visceral sense of community through the music — and what's more visceral than being part of sweaty human wave crashing toward the stage, singing and dancing and grinning til everything hurts — but also let us carry it out with us into the night, into our lives."
—*Rachel Weber*

Last Day on the Force. *Photographer unknown*

"When I think back over my favorite experiences at The Mr. Roboto Project, one that stands out as enjoyable and important — is a show I refused to enter. It was an evening in 1999 and The Weakerthans were playing. I had very little interest in this band outside of the Propagandhi connection and found them to be honestly a little revolting. I couldn't wrap my agitated, oppression-focused brain around the emotionally moving, exploratory lyrical style. I had become accustomed to a very high-energy, punky type of expression which employed overt references to radical struggle. I believed John K. Sampson had an obligation to use his privileged and popular status to promote some sort of social upheaval — and therefore [I] was uninterested in attending the show. I was hanging out on the front walk as I had agreed to assist in the duty of taking my daughter, Ray-gun, to see the band. She happened to love The Weakerthans at four years of age — influenced by my partner and co-parent Doug — who played the shit relentlessly in our home. I agreed to lurk around outside to give her breaks while he stayed in to enjoy the entire set. What turned my mind and makes this such a fond Roboto moment began with watching Ray-gun's smiling face cheering from atop Doug's shoulders as they entered, and continued as I watched the less familiar members of the crowd filter in. These were the folks I had seen around at shows and other events — folks I was curious about but had not much experience with so far. They also had smiling faces, and an energy and intensity to their presence. I clearly remember the crowd filing in between storefront windows filled with robot related décor — chattering and buzzing with that show-induced high so many of us have come to know and love. Something about experiencing this as an intentional outsider — at a venue I felt strong loyalty for — opened my mind to the finer details of this subculture I adore. A venue which I understood to exist to open access for bands to expose to a larger audience taught me how to end my habit of overlooking the less punchy and more subtle and complex musical poetry to be found in the underground. Thank you, Mr. Roboto, for teaching me how to consider myself an audience member to be educated — I couldn't have accepted that lesson from many places at such a self assured time in life — and I have worn the message well. I love you. Almost as much as I love The Weakerthans."

— *Kalie Pierce (Gunspiking)*

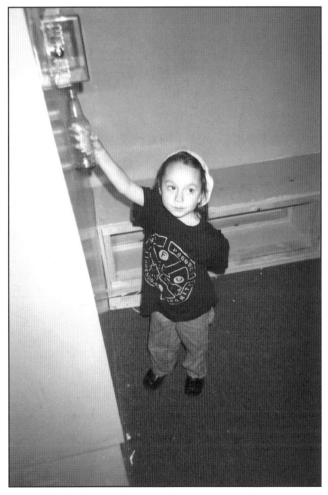

Ray-gun at Roboto. *Mike Q. Roth*

Trocar. *Shawn Brackbill*

Red Scare. *Shawn Brackbill*

Engine Down.
Shawn Brackbill

Engine Down. *Shawn Brackbill*

Orchid. *Shawn Brackbill*

"I remember this one show ... it was Orchid ... this was back before we had the PA mounted on the walls, so we just had the monitors on two folding chairs. The crowd that night was CRAZY, totally nuts, and I clearly remember a crazy pit and people diving off of the folding chairs with the speakers on them. Totally unsafe, insane and 100% AMAZING."
—Eric Meisberger (He Taught Me Lies, El Camino Club of SWPA, Soft Sickle, former member of the Roboto board of directors)

Orchid. *Shawn Brackbill*

Dillinger Four. *Shawn Brackbill*

"When Dillinger Four played the place was PACKED, so they played up on the "stage." It was also about 120 degrees in there. At the halfway point in their set, they wanted to take a smoke break, so they stopped playing, went outside, had a smoke break, came back in and finished their set."
— *Eric Meisberger*

Teddy Duchamp's Army. *Shawn Brackbill*

Selby Tigers. *Shawn Brackbill*

Selby Tigers. *Shawn Brackbill*

Pikadori. *Shawn Brackbill*

Pikadori. *John Herrington*

Annual Punx Picnic sponsored by Roboto. *Deanna Hitchcock*

Annual Punx Picnic sponsored by Roboto. *Deanna Hitchcock*

Ian Ryan and Swifty swim in the pond at Punx Picnic. *Mike Q. Roth*

The Fucking Champs. *Shawn Brackbill*

The Fucking Champs. *Shawn Brackbill*

The Dismemberment Plan. *Shawn Brackbill*

The Dismemberment Plan. *Shawn Brackbill*

Excelsior. *Shawn Brackbill*

Forstella Ford. *Shawn Brackbill*

"While not a specific memory, as a board member and frequent show goer, it was/is really awesome to watch young kids come into the Roboto/punk/what-have-you community and grow as people. As much as people and the media like to glorify the self-destructive nature of things associated with the punk aesthetic, I think Roboto really captures that spirit of individuality and recklessness of youth, but gives people an opportunity to steer it toward a positive creative outlet, whether it be through a band, booking shows, writing a zine, or just participating in some wacky do-it-yourself culture."
— Brian Gruetze

Ear to Ear. *Mike O. Roth*

Fate of Icarus. *Shawn Brackbill*

Le Shok. *Shawn Brackbill*

"... someone — I think it was Modey Lemon — played "Old Time Rock and Roll" for a world record length. Every time we thought it was about to end, they would go into YET ANOTHER reprise until they had been playing it for about 25 minutes. Rampant, absurd rock and roll hilarity!!"
— *Sarah Nokes-Malach*

Roboto had a few regular locals who stopped into shows over the years. YoYo was the most regular and long-running of them. She'd always announce her arrival, "YoYo's here!" and then almost without fail, claim that it was her birthday. She also claimed that once everyone picked her up and carried her around while singing "Happy Birthday." I have never heard third party confirmation of this story, but I like to believe that it actually happened."
—*Mike Q. Roth (He Taught Me Lies, former member of the Roboto board of directors)*

ADD Fest 3 in 2000. *Shawn Brackbill*

Microwaves. *Shawn Brackbill*

"Roboto had a few basic principles. One was that it was to be an all-ages space. To further that goal it was to be an alcohol and smoke free space. It was also to be a venue that promoted an anti-sexist, anti-racist, and anti-homophobic environment. This was to include more people, not to keep people out. These were always major points of contention with many folks who disliked the space as a result. People often focused on what you couldn't do there. I think they missed the point of what you could do there. You could form your own band and book your own shows there. You could run for the board of directors. It was an empty room that you could create something in if you chose."
— Ian Ryan

Microwaves. *Shawn Brackbill*

Microwaves. *Shawn Brackbill*

Teddy Duchamp's Army. *Shawn Brackbill*

Party of Helicopters. *Shawn Brackbill*

"Circle pitting barefoot. Why did I ever think that was a reasonable decision?"
— *Jen Briselli*

A circle pit. *Brad Quartuccio*

The Rapture. *Shawn Brackbill*

GoGoGo Airheart. *Shawn Brackbill*

Engine Down. *Shawn Brackbill*

Engine Down. *Shawn Brackbill*

Q and Not U. *Shawn Brackbill*

Q and Not U. *Shawn Brackbill*

Q and Not U. *Shawn Brackbill*

The Locust. *Shawn Brackbill*

The Locust. *Shawn Brackbill*

Pink and Brown. *Brad Quartuccio*

Arab On Radar. *Shawn Brackbill*

Red Monkey. *Shawn Brackbill*

The Cherry Valance. *Shawn Brackbill*

The Cherry Valance. *Shawn Brackbill*

Tight Bros From Way Back When. *Shawn Brackbill*

Roboto II before the stage was built.
Mike O. Roth

"Control show at Roboto II where there were like 7 kids and we circle pitted around the stage."
—*Brian Gruetze*

Roboto II. *Mike O. Roth*

Two Man Advantage. *Brad Quartuccio*

"... and this random woman wandering into a show blasted out of her mind and sparechanging everyone throughout the show, then walking up to Dropdead in between songs and saying "I don't belong here" and Bob, the singer, saying "You belong here, you are a human being."
—*Rachel Courtney*

He Taught Me Lies at Roboto II. *Deanna Hitchcock*

Pikadori at Roboto II. *Shawn Brackbill*

"When Roboto 2 got shut during that Creation Is Crucfixion show, I remember picking up the PA and walking down to the original space and continuing the show there. There a was a block-long parade of show-goers, band members and folks carrying equipment."
—*Eric Meisberger*

Alpha Control Group C at Roboto II. *Shawn Brackbill*

Dianogah at Roboto II. *Shawn Brackbill*

Les Savy Fav at Roboto II. *Shawn Brackbill*

"Roboto II was so weird and big. Some band moved benches around to fence in the crowd and keep them in a smaller space in front of the stage, so they wouldn't be so spread out, and that actually worked pretty well."
—*Rachel Courtney*

The Apes at Roboto II. *Shawn Brackbill*

"The infamous 9 Shocks Terror incident — Bill and I drove Molotov Cocktail, who were touring with Ratos de Porao, from Brazil, to the show from NYC. There was a snowstorm and everyone was late (the opener, Crucial Unit, had played an hour before we got there), and the show had to be over at 11 at the absolute latest. Molotov played, and then Ratos played and were done at about 10:30. 9 Shocks were told that they could play another show in a couple of weeks, and were told that the plug was being pulled on them at 11, but they insisted on playing and took 25 minutes to set up. As 11 approached (like, 1 song in!) their bass player, Tony Erba, said he'd kill anyone who turned off the PA. The PA was turned off anyway, Tony threw a mic stand into the audience and called some female audience members "cunts" and told one to "shut her piehole (!)" when they told him to chill out. Then he started whining about how they drove 3 whole hours to get to the show (which meant they left Cleveland around the time the show was supposed to start). He was worried that his other band's show, set up by the same promoter, would be cancelled, and the promoter told him he'd still do it if Tony apologized to the women he yelled at, but he would not."
— *Rachel Courtney*

Anti-Flag. *Shawn Brackbill*

Anti-Flag. *Shawn Brackbill*

Teddy Duchamp's Army. *John Herrington*

"The first time I went, I took a cab there with my college friend who was also into cool music, because we had no idea where Wilkinsburg was. Later, I remember very nearly getting egged by some neighborhood kids on Halloween, because I got lost on the way to a show at the new location that held Roboto II. But once the locations became familiar, and the faces started to have names, I felt more at home there than I ever did in my college dorm."
— *Shahrzad Samadzadeh*

Denali. *Shawn Brackbill*

Whatever It Takes. *Shawn Brackbill*

This Bike is a Pipebomb. *Brad Quartuccio*

"Worst shows were always (for me) bands from out of town that didn't understand what Roboto was trying to do and how much effort was involved in keeping that space going through cooperation with the community. Roboto made amazing things happen with scant resources and it was always frustrating when bands didn't respect that— showing up late and being bummed when they had to cut their set short no matter how many times they'd been told there was a hard curfew (Tony Erba throwing a fit and having the power pulled when they didn't want to go on until 10 and the show had to be over, Remingtin taking an hour and a half to plug all their gear in then taking it all down and driving back to Columbus because they spent their whole time slot setting up) but most of the time bands were amazed to be in such a positive space in front of such a receptive and earnest audience."
—*Brian Watson*

Re-doing the floors. *Mike Q. Roth*

"When the floor needed replaced, I helped rip up a bunch of the old boards and put down the new floor with Q and DHD. Mikey B ripped up the carpet the night before pretty much by himself."
—*Eric Meisberger*

An Albatross.
Charissa Hamilton-Gribenas

An Albatross. *Charissa Hamilton-Gribenas*

"The week after my mom died, Total Fury played at Roboto. After dealing with the funeral and all the grief and family for a week I felt like I needed to get out for an evening and go to a show. They were amazing. I watched the bass player run UP THE WALL. Literally. That show was really special."
—*Eric Meisberger*

Corpus Christie. *Chris Boarts Larson*

Intense Youth! *Missy Wright*

"Regurgitation Summer. Hellnation show with the iced tea drinking competition beforehand. Garbage cans full of vomit. Ian drank the most tea, was the only one not to puke and still play a killer set. Out of towners thinking that we were idiots."
—Zak Kovalcik *(Krooked Grind, Suburban Death Machine, Sequoia)*

Tragedy. *Chris Boarts Larson*

"I remember the time Tragedy played and you could see the floor just bouncing up and down. It was kind of terrifying."
—*Eric Meisberger*

Tragedy. *Chris Boarts Larson*

"Then there was the time when TOTALLY AWESOME DUDES and CROWD DETERRENT had their big showdown at what I recall was titled "Unity Fest" or something. The specifics of the "beef" aren't really that interesting, but what clearly sticks out in my mind were when Mike and John Kasunic, both teenagers at the time, were the only real recipients of violence and they really weren't even involved with TAD, just holding guitars."
—*Greg Mantooth (Warzone Womyn, Slices, former member of the Roboto board of directors)*

Iced tea funnel. *Charissa Hamilton-Gribenas*

Aphasia. *Missy Wright*

"The tea-drinking contest at the Voetsek/Brody's Militia gig in like '02 was insane. Ian rolled in with at least two gallons of Turner's. He was crowned the winner, because he drank almost 1 gallon and was the only one not to puke all over the place. Someone from Brody's Militia was overheard saying that in his 20 years of punk, he had never witnessed anything so asinine. Pretty much summed up the spirit of the times."

— Intense Andy Perlman (Intense Youth!, Brian Handle, Fuckedupmess, Soft Sickle)

RAMBO. *Missy Wright*

"When I was on the board, once I had to watch a show that had a sort of skinhead band on the bill. The guys in the band all seemed like good folks (no boneheads) and they all had the skin style. At the time, the beauty parlor next door was owned by a woman whose son, Ronny, was 9 at the time. He would come over and hang out at the space. I remember, for whatever reason, Ronny and I were sitting on the stage ... up, behind the band ... playing cards. So when folks walked in, they saw 4 skinheads playing music, and behind them on stage was a white guy with a big beard and a nine-year old African-American kid playing cards."

—*Eric Meisberger*

Jesus vs. the Easter Bunny at the Easter RAMBO show. *Missy Wright*

"One of my favorite Roboto memories is from when I was living in Allentown, PA, and a crew of us made the roadtrip across the state for the RAMBO/Crucial Unit/Caustic Christ/Krooked Grind show on Easter of 2003. We rolled into town and went over to Joe Hammer where numerous props were being built while Aus-Rotten blasted over the stereo in the street. The show was insane, featuring a Jesus and the Disciples versus the Easter Bunnies theme.

The thing that blew me away the most, honestly, was how many women were dancing and getting involved at the show. It was a lot different than what I was experiencing at home, and I remember raving for weeks to friends in Allentown about the 'Pittsburgh ladies circle pit brigade,' as I dubbed them."

—*Kyle Folsom (former member of the Roboto board of directors)*

Kylesa. *Chris Boarts Larson*

Aphasia. *Chris Boarts Larson*

"Seeing all my friends sing all the words at the last Io show and feeling so incredibly honored to have been a part of that, feeling the give and take between the band and the audience as though it was one living thing, not a performance ..."
—Brian Watson

Io. *Chris Boarts Larson*

Krooked Grind. *Chris Boarts Larson*

Krooked Grind. *Chris Boarts Larson*

Aphasia. *Chris Boarts Larson*

"It's difficult to pick a single moment or even a handful of stand-out moments. I think what made the early years of Roboto exciting for me was the prevailing attitude conveyed by the people that attended the shows. I feel like often the crowd was there to entertain the bands just as much as the bands were there to entertain the crowd. I think a lot of people wanted touring bands to feel welcome and to leave our city with a positive impression. This sometimes resulted in shows with 10 people in attendance being legendary and memorable in some of our minds."
— Ian Ryan

"There was a span of a month or so in winter 2000/2001 where Roboto hosted Crispus Attucks, The Degenerics, Tear It Up and Tragedy (maybe not in that order). It was a great time to be alive."
— *Intense Andy Perlman*

Caustic Christ.
Chris Boarts Larson

Crucial Unit.
Chris Boarts Larson

"sometime in 2002? The first time I saw Crucial Unit. Not the first time I had been to Roboto, but probably the first time I understood why it was great."
—*Brian Paull*

"Department of bad ideas ... dumping a tub of ice water on top of Justin during a Crucial Unit set. Forgetting to tell Bolam to get his pedals off the floor."
— Ryan Hughes

Crucial Unit. *Chris Boarts Larson*

"August '03, Crucial Unit's homecoming show. My first time in the city/at Roboto. I was blown away at the space/community, Pittsburgh looked like such a positive and progressive place to me! Coming from Buffalo, Pittsburgh was practically Portland."
—Christopher Schwarzott

Ian Ryan. *Missy Wright*

"There was a period of time where pretty much any band elicited a pretty outrageous response from the crowd. I won't say that some of those bands were "mediocre," but going back and listening to some of those records, it confuses me a little as to why we were tearing up the carpets and swinging from the rafters when we saw them live. Probably not as confused as the actual bands were when they saw us doing such things in response to their music."
—*Greg Mantooth*

Ian on a wall of death. *Missy Wright*

Crucial Unit. *Missy Wright*

Crucial Unit. *Missy Wright*

Greg Mantooth on thrash throne. *Missy Wright*

I ride the thrash throne.
Q yells get off the rafters
millions of rug burns.
— *Greg Mantooth (haiku written for ADD fest VI)*

"Bathtub Shitter was playing on a Thursday with three other bands. 7 p.m., none of the bands are there. 8 p.m., no Bathtub Shitter; Tunturi plays. 9 p.m., no Bathtub Shitter; Warzone Womyn play. 9:30 p.m., Tumor Feast plays; Bathtub Shitter call the Roboto phone to say their van is broken and they'll catch a cab. Show is sold out, and the packed room of people all yell hello over the phone. 10:00 p.m., room is still packed, all present bands are finished playing, no Bathtub Shitter.

Roboto's standard stop time for weekday shows is 10:30 p.m.; it comes and goes, no Bathtub Shitter, Roboto is still packed with waiting people. Wilkinsburg's 11 p.m. curfew is looming. 10:45 p.m., Bathtub Shitter walk in after being rescued from a Cranberry Denny's by some local punks who realized that Japanese grindcore punks weren't the standard Denny's clientele. 10:57 p.m., they start playing and the room full of people goes berzerk. At 11:05 p.m., three songs in, they stop. Best show ever."
— *Dan Bidwa*

Greg Mantooth on thrash throne. *Missy Wright*

Krooked Grind. *Missy Wright*

"There was a period when any really good show would have a human pyramid—I remember seeing Forward and a pyramid formed in front of the singer and he absolutely flipped out with joy. There were also dueling walls of death and chicken fights with people riding on each others' shoulders. I think Minneapolis and maybe Denver tried to lay claim to inventing the thrash pyramid — yeah right! I actually have notes on some of the shows I've been to and according to that, the thrash pyramid was born at the Misery/Extinction of Mankind show on October 5, 2001. Beat that, Denver and Minneapolis!"
—*Rachel Courtney*

Thrash pyramid. *Missy Wright*

Thrash pyramid. *Missy Wright*

Caustic Christ. *Missy Wright*

Behind Enemy Lines. *Shawn Brackbill*

Wall of death. *Charissa Hamilton-Gribenas*

Crucial Unit. *Charissa Hamilton-Gribenas*

Sun Tornado. *Shawn Brackbill*

"At an lo gig, some of us jokesters decided it would be funny to yell the name of the old Pittsburgh Oi group The Sussed for the entire duration of the show. Not sure why, but it seemed like a good idea at the time."
— *Intense Andy Perlman*

Vivisick and a thrash pyramid. *Missy Wright*

"When my friends and I were in high school in northeast Ohio, some of our older friends had told us that punks in Pittsburgh wouldn't talk to you until they had "baptized" you in iced tea. When I eventually made it to Roboto a year or so later, I was happy that a drunk Ed Steck just spit on my leg while giving me a Brain Handle flier instead. (It was cool. He cleaned it off afterward.)"
— *Gregory Murray*

Fucked Up and Greg Mantooth on a pogo stick. *Missy Wright*

"I was 19 and had just moved to Pittsburgh for school. My first show at Roboto was DS-13, Crucial Unit, and Caustic Christ a few weeks after I had arrived. I hadn't been to that many shows during my formative punk years due to being somewhat isolated in the suburbs of Philadelphia. There was a circle pit and it blew my damn mind. I tried to act real cool, like it was no big thing, like I had seen this kind of thing like a billion times before. I bought some shitty grindcore records from the Havoc distro and was equally stoked."
—Greg Mantooth

Fucked Up. *Missy Wright*

Wrangler Brutes.
Charissa Hamilton-Gribenas

Takaru. *Charissa Hamilton-Gribenas*

"I remember the first Life at These Speeds tour through Pittsburgh. What I did NOT remember was how to get to the Roboto Project. We found this out a solid half an hour after the show started when I realized we had gone down Wood in the opposite direction. We did make it. Eventually. You cannot go home again (without asking for directions)."
—Alan Dubinsky (Life at These Speeds)

Stencilling robots. *Mike Q. Roth*

the sea, like lead. *Charissa Hamilton-Gribenas*

"My number one favorite Roboto event is always ADD Fest. Forever. All of them. In 2004, I was working at an office with a fabulous color printer and thought I should really make good use of it. This was during the spell when the infamous messageboard was still tied in with Roboto, and when Jeremy Hedges' posting accounted for probably 50% of all posts on there. His band (the sea, like lead) was playing ADD that year, and good lord did they take themselves seriously (I say this with nothing but love in my heart for those fellas, 2/3 of whom have lived with me at some point). I don't stand by the idea of internet personas being different from a real life persona, and that extends to internet jokes becoming real life jokes ... and so for the 2004 ADD Fest, fellow board poster Jeff Schreck and I made masks of Jeremy Hedges' face. As they were setting up to play, we quietly passed them around to everybody in the room, and as soon as they began the first song, everybody put their masks on. Absurd and wonderful."
—*Emma Rehm*

the sea, like lead. *Charissa Hamilton-Gribenas*

Jeremy Hedges mask. *Charissa Hamilton-Gribenas*

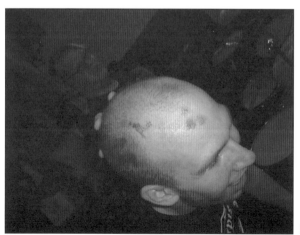
Greg Mantooth's rugburned head. *Mike O. Roth*

At the Multi-Tool. *Deanna Hitchcock*

He Taught Me Lies at the Multi-Tool. *Mike Q. Roth*

Modey Lemon. *Charissa Hamilton-Gribenas*

"... Feeling like a part of a community of musicians and artists that really encouraged each other and feeling inspired every time I attended the space ... Feeling like the best music in the world was made by my best friends and not caring if anyone beyond those walls had ever heard of any of us ... Feeling like we really could change the world around us, little by little. I have really longed for a community like that ever since, and I hope that people will keep in mind how important and real that environment is compared to virtual communities like Facebook and message boards. I miss Pittsburgh!"
—Brian Watson

Aftermath of flooding at Roboto. *Mike Q. Roth*

"Now, any reader knows that all bands were limited to a 10-minute timespan, and "Trapped Under Ice" is 4:05 on the album incarnation. Considering the length of most Hovland jams, we were cutting it close. We ripped into the song and I gave it my best to the audience, many of whom were quite literally trapped indoors due to the freezing conditions outside. I have no idea how it all sounded in retrospect, but energy levels were high and mighty fun was had. It all became unhinged at the very end, when we went over the time limit. Fail, the timekeeper, had flagged Corey, the guitar player, to our time infraction, pointing to a digital clock radio. Corey responded by raising the radio over his head and smashing it on the floor, while Mark, the drummer, jumped up on the drumset and yelled maniacally from adrenaline. By the time the smoke cleared, nobody in the audience seemed to take it all very well. As fun as it was, we had just succeeded in pretty much alienating ourselves from a friendly community of like minded individuals that undertook a mission I greatly admired. Fantastic!"
—*Jay Miller, recalling his guest spot during Hovland's set at ADD Fest 3*

Riistetyt. *Chris Boarts Larson*

"Few Da Real was one of the best/worst cover sets I've ever seen. Who ever thought that a struggling performance could be saved by a mid-act phone call from Rick Ta Life?"
— *Intense Andy Perlman*

"... I remember seeing a lot of amplifiers and a lot of DHD's hair."
—Evan Robinson (FLAK)

Behind Enemy Lines. *Christopher Schwarzott*

"Roboto had some problems with sewage flowing up and water flowing in. For weeks, my band had to tip-toe around a stinky sewage puddle in the basement that came up from the drain. I kept offering band members money to stick their hands in it or to straddle it while making obscene gestures. A couple years later, an underground pipe broke on Wood St. and our equipment got submerged in muddy water."
— *Timothy Williams (Alpha Control Group C, Arrivals and Departures, Abysme)*

Brain Handle. *Missy Wright*

"Brain Handle's first gig. We sounded like a hot mess. Family Circus was drunk and fell off a chair directly onto a Brita water pitcher, smashing it with his chest. After the performance, he was very adamant about finding the perpetrator who broke his pitcher."
— *Intense Andy Perlman*

Gouka. *Christopher Schwarzott*

Suburban Death Machine. *Missy Wright*

"In spring of 2005, we (the sea, like lead) played a show with Oxford Collapse — this was before they were on Sub Pop, and I think it was their first show in Pittsburgh. It was a Friday or Saturday night, it was a three-band show, it was over pretty early. This was the period when there was often a marauding group of teens and pre-teens around Wood Street at a certain hour of the evening, making lots of noise and sometimes harassing people. Right after the show ended, we could hear a loud group of kids getting closer and closer. We realized they were about to come into Roboto. It was a little intimidating — this was a big, screaming bunch of teenagers. A few guys stood up against the door and tried to block them from coming in for fear they were about to start a fight, but there were so many kids, they pushed it open. They all filed in — probably 20 to 30 of them — yelling stuff like 'PARTY AT THE ROBOT!' One had a video camera. Finally they were all inside, and we were all standing there kinda looking at them, and one of them said 'Aw, there's nothing going on here!' and they all left."
— Andy Mulkerin (the sea, like lead)

Suburban Death Machine. *Christopher Schwarzott*

"I remember a show Ian Ryan set up where a whole band showed up uninvited. They had trainhopped there with no equipment of any kind, not even guitars. They asked to play the show and asked if they could borrow another band's equipment, which was not going to happen. Then they asked to be let in for free to watch the show. Finally they stood outside panhandling for admission, saying, 'We ASKED if we could play and we ASKED if we could get in for free but they wouldn't let us!' Later that night they were making fun of Caustic Christ for having a van."
—*Rachel Courtney*

Government Warning. *Missy Wright*

Allies. *Christopher Schwarzott*

"I remember the time there was an iced tea drinking contest before a show, and I got there in time for the aftermath — iced tea puke all over the sidewalk. I think Ian won because he was the only one who didn't throw up."
— *Rachel Courtney*

Brain Handle. *Christopher Schwarzott*

Build Your Weapons. *Brad Quartuccio*

Isha & Zetta. *Brad Quartuccio*

Warzone Womyn.
Missy Wright

"Being a young punk in northeast Ohio, I had heard of Roboto when I was in high school. In September 2005, when I came to school at Pitt, one of the first things I did was head out to Roboto to see MDC play, who were kind of pathetic and terrible. ("What do you want to hear next?" Tired old punk song. "What do you want to hear next?" Fifty minutes goes by.) I got on the 71C in Oakland and took it to where I later learned was East Liberty. I went inside a Rite Aid to ask where Wood Street was, and the cashier told me that there was a Wood Street in Wilkinsburg and that I should just walk up Penn Avenue until I came to it. So I did. I walked for about forty or fifty minutes in my 14-eyed Doc Martens until I got there. Later, Corey Lyons told me that he had seen me walking down Penn and would have offered me a ride if he had known I was going to Roboto. This isn't much of a story, but it's what happened the first time I went to Roboto while I was living in Pittsburgh."
— *Gregory Murray*

He Taught Me Lies.
Charissa Hamilton-Gribenas

Flotilla Way. *Charissa Hamilton-Gribenas*

"The hardcore punk scene in the late 1990s was not at all an enclave of racial, gender, or even economic diversity. And of course it must be said that attending to issues of diversity require more than merely counting heads. But, when I think back to that day when Eric, Q, and Deanna gathered a bunch of us to discuss launching the Mr. Roboto Project, it struck me as unique and important that more than a third of the people in the room, and more than a third of the founding members were women. That might not sound significant to someone unfamiliar with the gender divide within the national hardcore punk scene. But this was absolutely atypical."
—Jessica Ghilani *(former member of the Roboto board of directors)*

Lorna Doom. *Mike Q. Roth*

Weird Paul. *Brad Quartuccio*

Isha & Zetta. *Mike Q. Roth*

"The first time I came to Roboto I was living in NYC and was roadie-ing for Broken, who were touring with Aus-Rotten. I was really impressed with the space and the scene — there were a lot of women, it didn't revolve around alcohol, people were going nuts for the bands, and wasn't very fashiony. Everyone was just wearing jeans and t-shirts. I loved the idea of a space similar to ABC No Rio in New York, but ABC only had one show a week and Roboto had several. I think I saw the possibilities that living in a city with a lower cost of living opens up, the ability to easily rent or even buy spaces to do DIY music and art, and I was really attracted to that."
—*Rachel Courtney*

Rick Gribenas. *Charissa Hamilton-Gribenas*

Roboto walls. *Christopher Schwarzott*

Caustic Christ. *Missy Wright* Young Enough to Sell (Neil Young cover band). *Missy Wright*

"I never made it out to Roboto all that much, I was so young back then that I didn't even realize what was going around me. All these people were part of something I didn't even know existed, to me at the time I thought it was just another place to see music. A few years later Coal Miner was asked to play what would be the last ADD Fest at the Wilkinsburg location, I didn't know what to think of it but after a quick conversation with Joel Grimes, he convinced me it was a show I should not pass up. On the day of the show we arrive and the place is packed with familiar and unfamiliar faces, and during the show I remember thinking to myself "nobody has heard of these bands, everyone is watching all the bands, no one is outside, these people actually give a fuck" this is when I first realized Roboto is more than just a venue, it's a community of people who give a fuck."
—*Maxx Gregg (Coal Miner, Allies)*

Sunday Morning Einsteins.
Missy Wright

FLAK. *Missy Wright*

Kim Phuc. *Missy Wright*

Dirty Faces. *Christopher Schwarzott*

Brain Handle. *Missy Wright*

Brain Handle. *Christopher Schwarzott*

Warzone Womyn. *Missy Wright*

In Aprill 2011, four women (Alyssa Truszkowski, former Roboto board member; Missy Wright, member; Jen Briselli, former Roboto board member; Holly Smith, singer, Broken Neck) got together to discuss the way gender was addressed within Roboto. These are excerpts from that conversation.

* * *

Alyssa: How did the official anti-sexist aims of Roboto match the actual culture at any given show? Punk and hardcore are viewed by some as subcultures that aren't necessarily friendly to women in general; do you agree or disagree with this idea, and how did Roboto fit into that cultural norm?

Missy: I don't think the world in general is really warm to women, I really don't think that. I mean, I constantly feel like there's a war on women out there, to be honest. And so I don't think Roboto is necessarily any different … I don't think that punk and hardcore is necessarily worse in a lot of ways. I mean, lyrically, and stuff like that it can be, but, to be honest, I think that the world really … we're second-class citizens. And I don't think punk and hardcore treats us any differently.

Jen: I think movements in the punk scene, and Roboto's scene specifically, or even movements that have happened over the larger course of time and society — they've just made it less OK to be overt about the feelings people have.

Missy: Right.

Jen: But those feelings are still there, for a lot of people they're bred into them from being brought up from such a young age to interact with women in the way that people do. So, I don't think that Roboto's any different than any other community. It's just that … there are pockets of society where it's made more or less OK to be outwardly for or against certain things. Versus in Roboto, where it's less OK to express sexist feelings. But, they still exist.

Missy: They still existed, with people that … you knew they thought it, you know they won't say it in front of you because, well, the shit will hit the fan, but you know that it's there. Because that's how it is in the world.

Holly: And, well, just look at who it's made up of. It's all white, privileged males at shows. So, as much as we may like to think the ones that are there are a little bit more enlightened, they're not.

Missy: They're still white privileged males who don't question that privilege.

Broken Neck. *Sarah Carr*

Holly: I was still having to explain to guys why I don't want to be called "female-fronted hardcore" or, you know, "girl vocals." They don't understand — "Well, that's what it is." And it's like, I'm not a novelty. This isn't a subgenre — "female hardcore." It's just hardcore.

Missy: Yes, you happen to be a woman, but it's hardcore.

Holly: They say, "Well, I like chick singers" and it's like, are you serious?

Missy: They're the same people who don't understand that saying "she's a good guitar player for a woman" is not a compliment.

Holly: And it's just always so shocking to me, when [guys are] like, "Oh, you'd like that band, there's a girl in that band." Are you kidding me? Like I'm expected to like every band that has a girl singer just because I am one.

Alyssa: I will say that when I first moved out to Pittsburgh and when I first started to get to know some of the people at Roboto ... the bands that I liked that did have women participants, they actually knew about. And that was so weird to me. That's such a small part of it, but it was for some reason surprising. I just thought it was cool, just different from working at the radio station at Pitt; that's a huge thing there. Gender stuff usually is one of the categories that comes up when you're talking about a band or whatever.

* * *

Jen: I really liked that most of the people I interacted with in Roboto weren't just interested in censoring somebody, but actually having a dialogue about why your privilege makes you act the way you do, or why this is not acceptable to say. It wasn't just about "you're not allowed to use this word," it was more about "what's wrong with wanting to use the word in the first place." And I felt that definitely died off again toward the end, but a lot of things about Roboto did just because of the way that things worked out. But during the years that I was very active, I felt that was one of the things as a woman, I felt most respected about, was because people seemed more interested in making sure guys learned why something wasn't cool, as opposed to "just don't say this."

And remember the word "fag," there was such a giant fiasco with that, for a couple years there, and I remember how I would be livid for entire days because I would be so frustrated with how idiotic people were, but there were people who actually thought it was worthwhile to actually talk about, well, "I don't mean the word that way, it's just a derogatory term I use for my friends," and then to actually make the effort to have the discussion about why using it is a derogatory term in the first place. But it was like ... This is the first institution I've ever been a part of that actually wanted to have that conversation or dialogue. Now, how successful the dialogue has been? I think the jury is still out, but at least someone was trying.

Missy: But do you think that the people [were] less open to it toward the end? It seems like there's been a shift again, lately, toward the shocking. Trying to be shocking.

Jen: I think people are worn out, too.

Missy: Well yeah, and I think people — are you just sick of having this discussion over and over again with people that are not getting it? Or ... There's also been a movement of bands being more shocking and more, this sort of shift from the hyper-PC of the mid- to late '90s to going back to being super shocking again.

Jen: Absolutely. I would not be surprised if in a little bit of time, we see it go back the other way, and I do think that's a big part of it: a pendulum swing.

"I'm in law school now, and I list The Mr. Roboto Project on my resume under "Community Activities." Sometimes, big-time corporate lawyers ask me what it is, and I'm always super stoked to have a chance to talk about it."
— Gregory Murray

Brain Handle. *Christopher Schwarzott*

Meltdown. *Brad Quartuccio*

"Fleas and Lice were playing Roboto and my plan was to go to the show and then directly after, get in a car with my friend Carlin to drive to Boston. They played and it ruled, the punks went crazy! After the show I grabbed my backpack and placed in on the ground for a minute before loading up the car. We drove all the way to Allentown, Pa and opened up the trunk. It smelled awful and we couldn't figure it out at first, but when I grabbed my soggy backpack, I knew what it was. When I sat the bag on the ground outside of Roboto, I unknowingly dropped it in a puddle of piss! It sucked, but I couldn't be that mad ... afterall, I was just at a Fleas and Lice show and pissing in public is expected, right?"
—*Leanne O'Connor*

Soft Sickle and Mike Q. Roth performing as Ignition during "Classic Dischord Band Night."
Brad Quartuccio

Unreal City. *Tanner Douglass*

"Having to watch shows is probably universally regarded as being a drag at least some of the time by anyone who served on the board of directors. They were the best of times. They were the worst of times. Surprisingly enough, sometimes they were one in the same. At one show I was watching, some band somehow had perfected the "Seinfeld Bass Sound" without them seemingly knowing it. This delighted me to no end and lifted my spirits on a cold, late December evening. When they asked if everyone could hear everything OK, I told them that we could use a little more bass in the mix. They obliged and I basked in all its glory."
— Greg Mantooth

Gray Ghost. *Tanner Douglass*

Slices. *Dan Gamble*

The Endless Blockade. *Dan Gamble*

"Some of the best memories I have of the space are of shows that I don't even remember who played. There would be 20 people there on a cold March night, and I'd either be watching the show, or in a band playing, or just out to support ... and there was this great feeling of comfort. I always felt like that room was like my living room."
—*Eric Meisberger*

Hellnation. *Dan Gamble*

Coffins. *Tanner Douglass*

"I don't know where I'd be with my life now if we hadn't done Roboto. Because of my involvement on the board of directors at Roboto, I went on to be on other boards, I made connections which have given me some pretty great employment opportunities over the last decade. I went on to have bands that actually toured and put out records. I met some of the most amazing people. It's possible something else might have come along, but I feel like if we hadn't taken that chance back then, my life just wouldn't be as satisfying as it has been."
—*Mike Q. Roth*

"One time there was this guy in the pit who was moshing really hard and intentionally trying to punch people in the face. All of a sudden the crowd acted as a whole to pass him from person to person and gently shoved him out the door."
—*Rachel Courtney*

Annihilation Time. *Tanner Douglass*

Masochrist. *Brad Quartuccio*

"All I ever had to worry about was finding my way to Roboto. If I wasn't meeting friends there, I'd know people by the time I'd leave and, nine times out of ten, they'd give you a ride back to your place or let you crash at theirs. That sense of camaraderie is my best memory about my teenage years."
— *Nathalie Bruce*

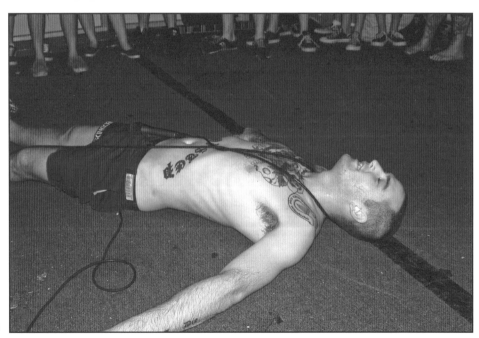

Ceremony. *Tanner Douglass*

"One time someone pushed a mesh backed baseball cap through the mailslot with a note written on it in Sharpie. It was about how they had come to the space on the wrong night for some show."
—Eric Meisberger

Castle. *Brad Quartuccio*

Hatred Surge. *Tanner Douglass*

"I always really enjoyed spending my time at Roboto. Going there on a Friday or Saturday night was so great because the bands were awesome, it was a familiar ritual, and most importantly, I always knew that I would see my friends there. We didn't even need to call each other to coordinate our plans; everyone just showed up. Even more important than the bands, I think, is the community that Roboto fosters. Everyone is intelligent, committed, and passionate (and into cool music), and that they all can get behind such a positive cause is very heartening."
— *Gregory Murray*

Hatred Surge. *Tanner Douglass*

Punch. *Tanner Douglass*

Cake made for ADD Fest 12 and Roboto's 10th Birthday Party.
Mike O. Roth

Front of Roboto during ADD Fest 12 and Roboto's 10th Birthday Party. *Mike O. Roth*

"It was my first time to the Roboto Project in Wilkinsburg. It was the first time I'd ever seen Broken Neck perform, and I got really excited and started into the pit. A few moments into letting my rage explode all over the small floor, I fell. I was on the ground for what seemed like hours, but it was actually only enough time to get a few good kicks to my stomach and skull. I was then abruptly pulled up by a helping hand. I exited the pit and stumbled outside into the cold winter air. My two friends followed me. They kept saying I didn't look too good, as I proceeded to pass out, and mumble a few unintelligible phrases. Not knowing what to do, they quickly carried me back into the steaming hot Roboto. A few friendly faces gathered around to see what had happened as people started to assume that I had alcohol poisoning. I was then carried outside yet again and put on the back of the drummer from Broken Neck's truck bed. They asked me and my friends if I had taken drugs or drank before the show. I hadn't, which swiftly led to the conclusion that I had a pretty serious concussion. My friend's mom picked me up and took me to the hospital, where I was until 4 o'clock in the morning. It was my second concussion in two weeks, and it was the best damn night of my life. I returned to Roboto many times after, having no shame while keeping up my addiction to music and rage."
— *Shannon Dailey*

Forfeit. *Tanner Douglass*

"What I liked best about Roboto was the reasonable hours. I've never understood "bar time" where you get home from work and have to wait hours and hours and then go to a show that starts at 10:30 p.m. and ends at 2:00 a.m. and you're miserable at work or school the next day. At Roboto, you'd be done at 10:30 p.m. and could get a good sleep so you'd be ready for more noise-making or show-going the next day."
— *Timothy Williams*

Shai Hulud. *Tanner Douglass*

Death Before Dishonor. *Tanner Douglass*

Path to Misery. *Tanner Douglass*

Brace War. *Tanner Douglass*

Ice Capades. *Tanner Douglass*

"One time I set up a show for a band called Defiance, Ohio at Roboto and right at 7, a group of street punks came through the door telling me how stoked they were to see Defiance. I told them that Defiance weren't playing, but Defiance, Ohio: a folk punk band from Bloomington. Street punks were bummed and called the Bloomington band 'posers' and left."
—*Leanne O'Connor*

Crowd during last shows at the original space.
Tanner Douglass

Bathroom. *Tanner Douglass*

"Knowing my toilet was a two minute drive away, was always comforting considering the bathroom at Roboto wasn't designed for people that were over 6 feet. I remember taking a wiz down there after somebody blew it up. It was terrible! So bad I couldnt help but laughing. As I zipped up and walked out I was still laughing about it, of course there ended up being a cute girl waiting outside. I never used the bathroom there again!"
— *Corey Lyons (Aus-Rotten, Caustic Christ, Kim Phuc)*

"I think the Unit had just returned from tour, and they had tons of cartons of warm soy milk with them. There was a drinking contest. I think I won, but I can't rightly recall. It sucked/kicked butt. Note to readers: Do not drink warm soy milk inside of a 100+ degree room, when your only bathroom option is the Roboto basement toilet."
— *Intense Andy Perlman*

"For some reason the graffiti in the bathroom at the Wilkinsburg space that said "in here it stinks like piss" has always stuck with me. I thought that should be the title of the Roboto book."
—*Rachel Courtney*

Merch table. *Tanner Douglass*

Crowd during last shows at the original space.
Tanner Douglass

Crowd during last shows at the original space.
Tanner Douglass

Crowd during last shows at the original space. *Christopher Schwarzott*

Year after year, Roboto was the home of hardcore/punk in Pittsburgh because it was more legit than a basement and not a lame rock club. Those of us who booked shows for international touring bands soon learned that the East Coast portions of their tours were usually planned around when they could play Roboto. Had it not been for the nature of the space and the dedication of all of those involved, Pittsburgh would not have been lucky enough to enjoy hosting so many great gigs for national and international groups.
—*Intense Andy Perlman*

The Endless Blockade. *Tanner Douglass*

The Endless Blockade. *Christopher Schwarzott*

The Endless Blockade. *Tanner Douglass*

Warzone Womyn. *Christopher Schwarzott*

Warzone Womyn. *Tanner Douglass*

Warzone Womyn. *Tanner Douglass*

"I could drop a million memories of specific experiences, but honestly I'd rather not. Those memories make up the fabric of years of my life, and that's a fabric I'd like to leave intact. We're lucky. Few people get to share their halcyon days of youth with such a large and diverse community, and even fewer can base it all on a particularly special location — let alone have it commemorated in a book." —*Shahrzad Samadzadeh*

ShowList

1999

11/12/99 – ADD Fest II: Kitty Pryde and the Shadowcats, Harm, There is No Name, Meisha, The El Camino Club of SWPA, Grand Buffet, Gary Bartz NTU Troop, Mistletoe, Land, The Viragoes, Crucial Unit, Jumbo, Disturbed Youth
11/28/99 – The Allied War Effort, The El Camino Club of SWPA
12/3/99 – Frodus, Jumbo, Mihaly
12/18/99 – Convocation of..., New Terror Class, Party of Helicoptors, Jumbo
12/19/99 – Dutchland Diesel, Grand Buffet, All-American Radio
12/31/99 – Disturbed Youth, TBA New Years Eve Bash!

2000

1/6/00 – Hovland, Control Group, 53rd State, Bryon Gill Trio
1/7/00 – Zentraedi, Pseudo Heroes, Joysticks, Pankration, Warlock
1/8/00 – Q & Not U, Darkest Hour, Gunspiking, Majority Rule
1/11/00 – Goliath!, Forstella Ford, Disturbed Youth, The Killing's Gotta Stop, Ese!
1/14/00 – Lycosa, the Last Forty Seconds, Crucial Unit, Fate of Icarus
1/19/00 – Winter Art Show w/music by Lis Harvey and Sam Wheeler
1/21/00 – DJ & Open Mic Night
1/22/00 – Miles to Failure, Creation is Crucifixion, (the) Control Group
1/26/00 – Kind of Like Spitting, Fred Weaver, All the Quiet, Grammar Radio
1/29/00 – Faraquet, Q and Not U, Tipping Canoe, Kolya, The Great Eastern
2/2/00 – FILM NIGHT: Imp-action + others
2/4/00 – Benefit for Roboto w/ Aus-Rotten, Disturbed Youth, Crucial Unit, Opposition
2/5/00 – Rock & Roll Bob, Brain Invaders, & Mud City Manglers
2/11/00 – Shoddy Puppet Company, El Camino Club of SWPA (last show), Looks Like Rain, Grand Buffet.
2/12/00 – Strong Intention, Crucial Unit, Steel Curtain, Sadis Euphoria
2/16/00 – Nuzzle, The Killing's Gotta Stop, Ese!, Whitford
2/18/00 – PUNK ROCK BINGO!
2/22/00 – Aloha, the Las Vegas, Grammar Rodeo
2/25/00 – Grand Buffet vs. Modey Lemon grudge match
2/26/00 – An Oxygen Auction, Control Group, Bad Blood, Pgh Free Improv Co.
2/28/00 – All-Scars, 53rd State, Null Set
3/1/00 – Milemarker, Kurt, The Killing's Gotta Stop, Ese!
3/2/00 – Franklin, Infinity, the Walnut St. Project
3/3/00 – Creta Bourzia, All the Quiet, the arco flute foundation
3/4/00 – Rough Trade Night: Pgh. bands doing all 80s post-punk and new-wave covers
3/5/00 – Paul Newman, Dianogah, Taking Pictures, The French Kicks
3/11/00 – Oxes, Lynx, Pittsburgh Dice, Weather Channel
3/12/00 – Rick Brown & Sue Garner, Boxstep, V for Vendetta, Anita Fix
3/17/00 – Sweep the Leg Johnny, Engine Down, Shelibound, Bald Rapunzel, The Great Eastern
3/18/00 – Isis, Cave In, The National Acrobat
3/19/00 – Karate, Ted Leo, The Las Vegas, The Killing's Gotta Stop Ese!
3/24/00 – Books for Prisoners Benefit featuring Opposition, Bryon Gill Trio, On the Outside, All Purpose Parade, Wrought with Sickness
3/25/00 – Metropolitan, Persons, All the Quiet, Infinity
3/26/00 – Bread and Water, Sadis Euphoria, the Melbas
3/29/00 – Good Clean Fun, Crucial Unit, Disturbed Youth, Steel Curtain
3/31/00 – Silver Tongued Devil, 53rd State, Bryan Gill Trio
4/1/00 – React, Broken, Bryon Gill Trio
4/5/00 – Discount, 53rd State, Crucial Unit
4/8/00 – The Iceburn Trio, Lenny Young & Jay Matula
4/9/00 – Les Savy Fav, The Apes, 53rd State
4/10/00 – Enemies, Pseudo Heroes, Ear to Ear
4/11/00 – Shipping News, Victory at Sea, Taking Pictures, All the Quiet
4/14/00 – RAMBO, No-Gos, Modey Lemon
4/15/00 – 90 Day Men, Brown System
4/15/00 – PUNK ROCK FLEA MARKET
4/16/00 – PUNK ROCK FLEA MARKET
4/18/00 – USV, Disturbed Youth, Crucial Unit, Died Trying
4/21/00 – Appleseed Cast, Rushmore, Fin Fang Foom, Ear to Ear
4/28/00 – Walls of Jericho, 12 Tribes, the Hope Conspiracy, A Life Once Lost
4/29/00 – Varsity, xSteel Curtainx, Sadis Euphoria, Fate of Icarus
5/1/00 – Bablicon, Arco Flute Foundation, Hovland

5/5/00 – A Better Tomorrow, World B, Gunspiking, Anihilation Uprising
5/6/00 – Q and Not U, Radio 4, The Great Eastern, Rich Mackin, Ted Leo, The Holy Childhood
5/9/00 – Tristeza, New Terror Class, Red Light
5/11/00 – Atom & His Package, Franklin
5/12/00 – Mach Tiver, Camera Obscura, (the) Control Group, the Killing's Gotta Stop Ese!
5/15/00 – Death Cab for Cutie, V for Vendetta, HARM
5/19/00 – Usurp Synapse, Jerome's Dream, Racebannon, Fate of Icarus
5/21/00 – Rodger that Houston, Ampline, The Las Vegas
5/22/00 – Atom Bomb Pocket Knife, The Rapture, Blunderbuss
5/25/00 – Time Flies, Count Me Out, Disturbed Youth (show cancelled)
5/27/00 – Cross My Heart, The Liars, Irwin, the Burning Sensations
5/28/00 – Amazing Transparent Man, Exclusion Principle, Dimstar 33
5/31/00 – FILM NIGHT: Big Girls by Sara McCool and a skateboard documentary
6/1/00 – Kill Sadie, The Great Eastern, Brown System
6/2/00 – Winterbrief, Mathlete, The Operators, Tourister
6/4/00 – 9 Shocks Terror, Strong Intention, Crucial Unit, Annihilation Uprising
6/6/00 – Anti-Product, Submission Hold, Gunspiking
6/7/00 – Golden, Human Brains, Control Group, Calibos
6/8/00 – The Most Secret Method, Teddy Duchamp's Army
6/11/00 – Onward to Mayhem, Party of Helicopters, Creta Bourzia, Bryan Gill Trio
6/12/00 – UNITY GATHERING: political activism meeting
6/15/00 – Aus-Rotten, Broken, World B
6/16/00 – Creation is Crucifixion, Fate of Icarus, Crucial Unit, Sadis Euphoria
6/17/00 – Wounds, Grand Buffet, The Enrique Slavadas Funtime Trio
6/18/00 – Foiling The Works, Sbitch, Anihilation Uprising, World B
6/20/00 – Eclipse of Eden, Neil Perry, Sadis Euphoria, Corpus Christie
6/24/00 – Looks like Rain, Gunspiking, The Chase, The Deadbeats
6/27/00 – Soophie Nun Squad, The Body, Sparrow
6/29/00 – Bane, Death By Stereo, Adamantium, Face Tomorrow
6/30/00 – Audience of One, Ruby Keeler, Pseudo Heroes
7/1/00 – Orchid, Red Scare, Forstella Ford, Paris at 2am
7/2/00 – Blood Brothers, True North
7/3/00 – ACOUSTIC NIGHT: Allison Williams, Coleman Lindberg, Lis Harvey, V for Vendetta, the Moves
7/7/00 – Pelt, Meisha, Land
7/8/00 – Bryon Gill Trio, Numerous Cats, Victor Vertigo
7/9/00 – DS-13, the Prophets, Killed in Action, Corpus Christie
7/10/00 – Engine Down, Razilia, the Great Eastern, Creta Bourzia
7/11/00 – Good Clean Fun, Majority Rule, Last Day on the Force
7/12/00 – Pinhead Circus, Qualm, Whatever it Takes, McCarthy Commission, The Melbas
7/16/00 – The Album Leaf, The Mercury Program, Fred Weaver, Mihaly
7/21/00 – Seven Days of Samsara, Daybreak, The Index, Lycosa, Cobra Kai
7/22/00 – Black Cat 13, Song of Zarathustra, Blow-up, Fate of Icarus
7/23/00 – Reversal of Man, Kill the Man Who Questions, Affront, Crucial Unit
7/24/00 – Dillinger Four, Silver Tongued Devil, Teddy Duchamp's Army
7/25/00 – Persons, HARM, Modey Lemon
7/28/00 – Milemarker, Mid Carson July, The Blackout Terror, Victor Vertigo
7/29/00 – Kung Fu Rick, To Dream of Autumn, Fate of Icarus, Crucial Unit
8/3/00 – Xibalba, The Square Mile, Tired Wheels, Last Day on the Force
8/4/00 – Circle Or, Philadelphia Experiment, A Better Tomorrow, All Purpose Parade
8/5/00 – Four Hundred Years, Pg. 99, Sutek Conspiracy, Circle of Dead Children
8/8/00 – Jen Wood, Walnut Street Project, Hovland
8/9/00 – Facedowninshit, Gunspiking, Jumbo
8/13/00 – The Crush, xSteel Curtainx, Teddy Duchamp's Army
8/16/00 – Zegota, Bodyhammer, Sparrow, World B
8/18/00 – Apocalipstik, All American Radio, MCDJ (aka Victor Vertigo)
8/19/00 – Landing, Land, Arco Flute Foundation
8/26/00 – Here Be Dragons zine release party w/ Disturbed Youth (last show), Crucial Unit, Anton Bordman, Ear to Ear
9/1/00 – Boiling Man, World B, Gunspiking
9/2/00 – Fat Day, Fate of Icarus, Party of Helicopters, Microwaves
9/3/00 – Kill Your Idols, the Movie Life, Corpus Christie, 3rd Place
9/5/00 – FREE WORKSHOP: hair cutting
9/8/00 – Benefit for RNC protest prisoners: Wrought with Sickness, Opposition
9/9/00 – Blinder, Punchline, Difference Makes One
9/10/00 – Punx Picnic
9/12/00 – World, Inferno Friendship Society, Radio 4, Selby Tigers, Pikadori
9/16/00 – Sadis Euphoria, Ear to Ear, Last Day on the Force,
9/17/00 – The Riffs, Corpus Christie
9/19/00 – The Jazz June, The Great Eastern, Teddy Duchamp's Army, The Operation, Last Day on the Force
9/21/00 – Freek
9/22/00 – The Weakerthans, Elliot, World B, Hedra
9/23/00 – A-set, the Chickens, Enon, Modey Lemon
9/26/00 – FREE WORKSHOP: soap making
9/27/00 – Subtracttozero, Aus-Rotten, Last Day on the Force
9/28/00 – The Fucking Champs, Excelsior, Jumbo
10/3/00 – Les Savy Fav, The Human Brains, Microwaves

10/7/00 – Black Cat 13, From Ashes Rise, Born Dead Icons, Crucial Unit
10/8/00 – Dismemberment Plan, Mercury Program, Microwaves, Get Hustle
10/10/00 – Botch, Sunshine, Pikadori, Tabula Rasa
10/13/00 – Haggard, Kitty Pryde and the Shadowcats, Corpus Christie
10/16/00 – Bright Eyes, A-set, Matt Suggs
10/19/00 – Us Against Them, Burning Sensations, Ear to Ear, The Code
10/20/00 – The Firebird Band, Haymarket Riot, Hero of a 100 Fights
10/22/00 – Strong Intention, Crucial Unit, Last Day on the Force, McCarthy Commission
10/25/00 – Tristeza, The Sissies, Rose of Sharon
10/26/00 – Barcelona, Tourister, HARM, Church Builder
10/29/00 – Ear to Ear, Grand Buffet, Fate of Icarus
11/1/00 – The Skag Boys, The Heinekins, Anti-Disbrigade, Dilznik, the Branigans, Liecus
11/4/00 – Hovland (record release), All the Quiet, Teddy Duchamp's Army, Tabula Rasa
11/6/00 – Le Shok, !!!, Choke City
11/8/00 – Vegetarian Chili Cookoff!! w/ (the) Control Group
11/9/00 – Steward, Girlboy Girl, A Boy Named Thor, Jen Turrell, HARM
11/10/00 – Harum Scarum, Aus-Rotten, Corpus Christie
11/11/00 – ADD FEST III: Roboto's 1 year anniversary
11/12/00 – Catharsis, Bloodpact
11/16/00 – The Body, Shut the Fuck Up, Last Day on the Force, Microwaves
11/19/00 – Ted Leo and the Pharmacists, Radio 4 (Show was cancelled because nobody came.)
11/20/00 – Grand Buffet, Microwaves, Weird Paul, Fizzies
11/25/00 – ex–NumberFive, Fifth Hour Hero, Creta Bourzia, Tabula Rasa
11/30/00 – The Cancer Conspiracy, The Logan Wish, Uncle Horse Embalmer, Fate of Icarus
12/8/00 – Photo show: Erin Zima, Charlotte Wright and Shawn Brackbill
12/15/00 – Pankration, Pg. 99, Cobra Kai, Fate of Icarus, Jumbo
12/17/00 – Tragedy, The Bodybag Romance
12/19/00 – Kill Your Idols, Strike Anywhere, American Nightmare, The Hope Conspiracy, Once and For All
12/21/00 – Circle of Dead Children, Red Sky, Nemo, August Prophecy, Decree
12/22/00 – The Devil Is Electric, This Bike Is A Pipebomb, David Dondero
12/28/00 – Kill the Slave Master, Glasseater, Arma Angelus, Sadis Euphoria, xSteel Curtainx

2001

1/2/01 – Cave In, Eulcid, Creta Bourzia, Tabula Rasa
1/3/01 – Flashbulb Memory, Ear to Ear, Majority Rule, Teddy Duchamp's Army, At Bay
1/6/01 – Ian Nagoski, Plea Circuits, Meisha, Neptune
1/7/01 – Women's Night: Women's Health discussion
1/12/01 – Crispus Attucks, What Lies Ahead, The Degenerics, Affront
1/13/01 – Strong Intention, The Control, Tear It Up, Caustic Christ
1/15/01 – Jerome's Dream, One AM Radio, Pseudo Heroes, Ear to Ear, The Great Clearing Off
1/19/01 – Art Opening
1/20/01 – Lite FM Night (local bands covering Lite FM songs): The Viragos, HARM, The Fizzies, Modey Lemon, Last Day on the Force, Hovland, Weird Paul
1/23/01 – The Lapse, Helms, Fred Weaver, Glow in the Dark
1/27/01 – The Red Room, There's Hope Yet, Fat Tony
1/28/01 – The Movie Life, Stryder, Punchline, Teddy Duchamp's Army
2/1/01 – Where Fear and Weapons Meet, Shark Attack, The Final Plan
2/2/01 – Here.Be.Dragons zine release show w/ The Four Seasons Boys, Ear to Ear, Pikadori
2/4/01 – Women's Night: Menstruation
2/10/01 – Upheaval, Kalibas, Fate of Icarus, Anthem Boy
2/11/01 – A Week In July, The Logan Wish
2/16/01 – Thomas Merton Center benefit: The Fireworks and the Stars, Glowinthedark, The Microwaves, Pikadori
2/18/01 – A Life Once Lost, Reign of Terror
2/23/01 – A Week In July, Hooray For Everything, Logan Wish, Rise Above
2/24/01 – Virginia Black Lung, Jumbo, Last Day on the Force, The Dusk, Teddy Duchamp's Army
2/25/01 – River City High, The Lawrence Arms, Walnut Street Project, Teddy Duchamp's Army
2/27/01 – Canyon, The Fireworks and the Stars
2/28/01 – Raw Pots Puppet show: Follow the White Rabbit
3/1/01 – Deathreat, Amebic Dissentary, Caustic Christ, Crucial Unit
3/3/01 – McCarthy Commission, Quit the Breathing, The Code, Tracer, The Citizens
3/4/01 – Zegota, World B, Malabaster, Eyes to Gomorrah
3/8/01 – United 51, Celebrity Roast, Once and for All, (the) Control Group
3/9/01 – Harikiri, Anodyne, Fate of Icarus, Sadis Euphoria
3/11/01 – 764-Hero, Kingsbury Max, Boxstep
3/12/01 – Party of Helicopters, Kepler, Choke City
3/13/01 – The Black Hand, Fortiori, The Awakening, Jumbo
3/16/01 – Teddy Duchamp's Army, Tabula Rasa, Last Day on the Force, Creta Bourzia
3/18/01 – Women's Night
3/19/01 – The Devil is Electric, Kitty Pryde, Blissful Idiots
3/22/01 – No info for show

3/23/01 – Allergic to Whores, Crucial Unit, McCarthy Commission, The Strain
3/25/01 – Killed in Action, Last Day on the Force, Drago, Tribe of the Hinayana
3/27/01 – Y, Strong Intention, Reign of Terror
3/28/01 – Yaphet Kotto, Volume 11, Io, Pleasure Forever
3/29/01 – HARM, Jane Speed, V for Vendetta, Kitty Pryde
3/30/01 – No info for show
3/31/01 – Silver Tongued Devil, Caustic Christ, Anti-Dis Brigade, BGA
4/1/01 – Enemymine, The Rapture, GoGoGo Airheart, Microwaves
4/2/01 – No info for show
4/4/01 – No info for show
4/7/01 – Q and Not U, Engine Down, Choke City, Io, Excelsior, Radio Four
4/8/01 – Harum Scarum, Gertrude, Behind Enemy Lines
4/9/01 – Martyr AD, Burnt by the Sun, Fate of Icarus, Decree
4/13/01 – A Benefit for Ron Wingrove w/ Last Day on the Force, Io, The Fireworks and the Stars, Pikadori, Aloha
4/14/01 – Glen Potential, Io, Tabula Rasa
4/15/01 – Vitamin X, Crucial Unit, The Chase
4/16/01 – Al Burian, Good Grief video showing, The Mohawk Maniacs
4/20/01 – Unfinished Symphonies, Frank Lloyd Wrong, 3 Generations of Atheists
4/21/01 – Lickgoldensky, Rise Above
4/27/01 – The Movie Life, Cooter, The Control, Lickgoldensky
5/1/01 – No info for show
5/3/01 – Creation is Crucifixion, The Oath, Total Fury, Kalibas, Circle of Dead Children, Sadis Euphoria
5/4/01 – Rich Mackin, World B, Phil Boyd and the Buffalords, Tribe of Hinyanna
5/6/01 – Abilene, Lovelife, The Others
5/11/01 – No info for show
5/12/01 – Hystera zine release w/ The Running Kind, Telesys, The Flying Seabees
5/13/01 – Sutek Conspiracy, Io, Gunspiking, World B
5/16/01 – Living Under Lies, Corpus Christie, Caustic Christ
5/17/01 – Atom and His Package, Har Mar Superstar, Grand Buffet
5/18/01 – Teddy Duchamp's Army, Pikadori, Tabula Rasa, Choke City, Hovland
5/19/01 – Good Clean Fun, Off Minor, Affront, Life Detecting Coffins
5/21/01 – Lovesick, Turn Around Norman, Kitty Pryde
5/23/01 – Second Story Man, City of Caterpillar, Creta Bourzia, Lay
5/26/01 – Mercury Program, Aloha, Fireworks and the Stars
5/29/01 – Pontius Pilate
5/30/01 – Bluetip, Fred Weaver, Teddy Duchamp's Army, Pikadori

6/1/01 – Red Room
6/3/01 – Crispus Attucks, Crucial Unit, Del Cielo, Reign of Terror, Hiretsukan
6/4/01 – Scott Smith, Tabula Rasa, Lauren Hospital, Where There Are Ghosts
6/7/01 – American Nightmare, The Citizens, Long Gone, The Code
6/8/01 – Pg 99, Majority Rule, Seven Days of Samsara, Io
6/9/01 – Tear It Up, Down In Flames, Affirmative Action Jackson, Last Day on the Force
6/11/01 – An Albatross, Io, John Ritter, Treeline Freeline
6/13/01 – Kite Flying Society, A Week In July, The Ezekial, The Logan Wish
6/14/01 – No info for show
6/15/01 – Tem Eyos Ki, Them of Delphi, Fortiori, The People's War
6/16/01 – Need New Body, Grand Buffet, Lord Sterling, Zombi
6/17/01 – Absurdis, Io, Jumbo, Choke City
6/18/01 – USV, Defacto Oppression, Caustic Christ, Tribe of the Hinyanna
6/20/01 – Landed, Conelrad, Commit Suicide
6/22/01 – Melee, Get Hustle, Reign of Terror, Orthrelm
6/24/01 – The Locust, The Control, Blowup, Choke City
6/26/01 – US Maple, Microwaves, Control Group
6/28/01 – Looks Like Rain, Shoddy Puppet Company, McCarthy Commission, Montag Conspiracy
6/30/01 – 53rd State (reunion), Sterling
7/2/01 – Strike Anywhere, Teddy Duchamp's Army, Youth Empowerment Project, Pikadori
7/3/01 – Video showing: Breaking the Spell
7/5/01 – Video showing: Pickaxe
7/6/01 – It Takes All Kinds, World B, Neotrope
7/7/01 – Goth Night: Sound Wars, Vampire Nation
7/9/01 – Diskonto, Behind Enemy Lines, Caustic Christ, Last Day on the Force
7/10/01 – What Happens Next, Life's Halt, Crucial Unit, Corpus Christie
7/11/01 – Lightning Bolt, Pink and Brown, Sightings
7/12/01 – Drowningman, Darkest Hour, When Dreams Die
7/14/01 – Last of the Juanitas, Tourettes Lautrec
7/15/01 – Don Austin, Killed in Action, The Awakening, Strange Division, Rise Above
7/16/01 – Malefaction, Backstabbers Inc, Zombi, Conelrad
7/17/01 – Kill Your Idols, American Nightmare, Fast Times, Tear It Up
7/18/01 – Harum Scarum, Control Group, Corpus Christie
7/20/01 – Pleasure Forever, Dean Swagger, Lay
7/21/01 – Assembly of God, Broken, Crucial Unit
7/22/01 – Ruination, Strong Intention, The Red Chord, John Ritter, Last Day on the Force
7/23/01 – Citizen Fish, Red Monkey, Counteraction

7/26/01 – This Machine Kills, Modey Lemon, DJ Fishfight and the Wizard of Oi
7/27/01 – Whatever It Takes, The Code, The Duplicators
7/28/01 – The Devil Is Electric, Pitfall, Crime Stories, Gunspiking
7/31/01 – The 6 Parts Seven
8/1/01 – Down In Flames
8/2/01 – Winterbrief, Girl Talk, Telesys, Churchbuilder
8/4/01 – Facedowninshit, Free Barrabas, Gunspiking, Fortiori
8/7/01 – Virginia Black Lung, 2am Revolution
8/8/01 – Lost Kids
8/9/01 – Whatever It Takes, Counteraction
8/10/01 – Apocolypstik, Io, All American Radio, Weatherfield
8/11/01 – Arab On Radar, Check Engine, Microwaves, Conelrad
8/12/01 – Sick of the Abuse, La Mantra de Fhiqria, Gunspiking
8/13/01 – Unholy Grave, Total Fuckin' Destruction, The Index, Cuttie, Behind Enemy Lines
8/14/01 – Rhythm of Black Lines
8/16/01 – From Ashes Rise, No Parade, Crucial Unit, Caustic Christ
8/17/01 – No info for show
8/18/01 – Shiner, Tabula Rasa
8/22/01 – Anthem 88, Behind Enemy Lines, Free Barabbas
8/23/01 – Rainy Day Regatta, Weird Paul and the Blissful Idiots, TBA
8/24/01 – 3 Ways Til Tuesday, Hooray for Everything, Came Crashing
8/25/01 – Ones and Zeros, I Farm, Io, Whatever It Takes
8/26/01 – The Body, El Camino Club of SWPA (reunion show), Denali
9/1/01 – Food Not Bombs benefit w/ Gunspiking, World B, Neotrope, Disinfectant, Full Catastrophe
9/6/01 – Keepsake
9/7/01 – DS-13, Crucial Unit, Caustic Christ
9/8/01 – Allergic to Whores
9/9/01 – Lickgoldensky
9/11/01 – Dismemberment Plan (cancelled), Har Mar Superstar, Song of Zarathrusa
9/12/01 – Lefty's Deceiver, Control Group, Mach Tiver, Pikadori
9/13/01 – The Owls
9/14/01 – Tight Bros from Way Back When, C Average, The Cherry Valance, Io
9/15/01 – Creation is Crucifixion, Sadis Euphoria, Conelrad
9/16/01 – They Live
9/17/01 – Phantom Limbs, Crucial Unit, Caustic Christ
9/20/01 – Pseudo Heroes, Mach Tiver, He Taught Me Lies
9/22/01 – FREEK, Forced Under, Negative Theory, Through the Shadows
9/28/01 – GC5, Tommy and the Terros, The Lashes, The Traditionals, My Drunk Uncle
9/29/01 – Honor System, Pikadori, The Ezekial, The Twirpentines
9/30/01 – Two Man Advantage, Phil A Sheo and the Goods, Leftover Crack, McCarthy Commission
10/2/01 – Strike Anywhere
10/4/01 – Butchies
10/5/01 – Roboto 1: Misery, Extinction of Mankind, Diallo, Behind Enemy Lines
10/5/01 – Roboto 2: David Turner show
10/12/01 – Destroyer, Summer Hymns, Cincinnatus
10/13/01 – Josh Pollock Birthday Party w/ Weird Paul
10/14/01 – Day Care Swindlers
10/15/01 – Dianogah
10/16/01 – Kill Devil Hills
10/19/01 – Tabula Rasa, Terminal Crash, Choke City
10/20/01 – Crispus Attucks, The Awakening, Free Barrabas
10/22/01 – Hella, Microwaves
10/23/01 – Palomar Sky Survey, The White Octave, The Logan Wish, Manifold Splendor
10/25/01 – Forstella Ford, Momento Mori, Pikadori, He Taught Me Lies
10/28/01 – Corn on Macabre
10/29/01 – Tracy and the Plastics
10/31/01 – Teddy Duchamp's Army, Shiver, Crucial Unit, Fin Fang Foom, World B
11/1/01 – Benefit for the Early Learning Center w/ AWOL, Midnight Murder, The Citizens, The Code, Whatever it Takes
11/3/01 – River City Rebels (didn't play), McCarthy Comission, Merry Fucking Christmas, Midnight Murder
11/4/01 – Les Savy Fav, !!! , The Apes
11/05/01 Piebald, Thursday, Lawrence Arms, Cancer Conspiracy, Whatever it Takes
11/9/01 – Counteraction, Weekend Warriors, The Ezekial, The Duplicators, Tommy Gutless
11/10/01 – Comin' Correct, Crowd Deterrent, My Drunk Uncle, Strength From Within, Down To None
11/11/01 – Milemarker
11/12/01 – Bane, Reach the Sky
11/16/01 – ADD Fest IV (Go Down Fighting release show)
11/17/01 – Boxstep, Elk City
11/18/01 – The Control
11/19/01 – Atmosphere
11/20/01 – Pikadori, He Taught Me Lies, Devil Is Electric, Puppy vs Dyslexia
11/24/01 – City of Caterpillar
11/26/01 – Converge, American Nightmare, Hope Conspiracy

11/27/01 – This Bike is a Pipe Bomb
11/30/01 – Power Ballad Night (local bands covering power ballads)
12/1/01 – Anti–Flag (live recording 2 shows)
12/8/01 – Merton Center Benefit w/ He Taught Me Lies, blowback, Giant Midget and various speakers against the war in Afghanistan
12/9/01 – RAMBO (Cops vs. Steelers theme), Momento Mori, Crucial Unit, Caustic Christ, Breaking Free
12/10/01 – Zegota, The Body, Behind Enemy Lines, He Taught Me Lies
12/11/01 – The Six Parts Seven
12/14/01 – Twelve Hour Turn, Pikadori, Io
12/17/01 – Creation Is Crucifixion (the night Roboto II got shut down)
12/18/01 – No info for show
12/19/01 – Liars
12/21/01 – Midnight Murder, The Strain, Corpus Christie, Caustic Christ, The Weekend Warriors, The Ezekial, The Duplicators
12/28/01 – Hudson Falcons, The GC5, My Drunk Uncle, Pig Iron, Counteraction

2002

1/3/02 – The Boils
1/4/02 – Agnes Wired For Sound
1/5/02 – Fortiori, Neotrope, TBA, He Taught Me Lies
1/6/02 – Denali, Pikadori
1/10/02 – World B, TBA. Honkey Dori, Pikadori, Fortiori
1/11/02 – Off Minor, Wolves, Tear It Up, The Deadly
1/12/02 – The Courier De Bois
1/13/02 – Armed With Intelligence, The Young Ones, Fortiori, Crowded Tombs
1/18/02 – Arco Flute Foundation, Neotrope, Pikadori
1/19/02 – Dalek, Blakk Squirrels
1/20/02 – King Django
1/21/02 – Creation is Crucifixion, Io, Microwaves, Nemo
1/26/02 – Wrought With Sickness, Memento Mori, Behind Enemy Lines, Intense Youth!
1/27/02 – The Tangent
1/31/02 – Paper Chase
2/1/02 – Whatever It Takes, Better Off Dead, The Ezekial, The Code, Merry Fucking Christmas
2/4/02 – Rape Discussion
2/7/02 – Liar's Academy
2/8/02 – Crimson Sweet, Corpus Christie, Counteraction
2/10/02 – Against Me
2/14/02 – Punk Prom
2/15/02 – Roboto Benefit w/ McCarthy Commission, Caufield Principle, Intense Youth, Caught Like Fire, He Taught Me Lies
2/19/02 – Tanka Ray
2/20/02 – Alexei and the Justins
2/22/02 – George Harrison tribute w/ Weekend Warriors, Modey Lemon, Evan Indifference, Counteraction, The Duplicators
2/23/02 – Free Barrabas, TBA, Spider Stigmatik, He Taught Me Lies
2/24/02 – My Hotel Year, A Week in July, Pikadori
2/26/02 – Courier de Bois
2/28/02 – May Day Benefit w/ Hip Criticals, Lorelei, He Taught Me Lies, Pikadori.
3/1/02 – Agnes Wired For Sound
3/2/02 – Caustic Christ (7" release), Crucial Unit, Behind Enemy Lines
3/3/02 – No info for show
3/4/02 – Atom and His Package, AM/FM, Weird Paul, Pretty Girls Make Graves
3/5/02 – Engine Down
3/6/02 – The Kants
3/7/02 – Close Call, The Duplicators
3/8/02 – RAMBO, Virginia Black Lung, This Day Forward, Intense Youth, Crowded Tombs
3/9/02 – Intense Youth, Counteraction, Tel-Star, My Life Tragic
3/12/02 – Mike Taylor and Lee Buford Art Show
3/13/02 – Dual Record Release: Behind Enemy Lines, Crucial Unit, Free Barabbas, Crowded Tombs
3/15/02 – Pikadori (CD release), He Taught Me Lies, Io, Alpha Control Group C
3/16/02 – Modey Lemon, Counteraction
3/20/02 – Blame Game, Aeros, Choke City, Conelrad
3/21/02 – The Owls
3/22/02 – Eyes To Gomorrah, TBA, 1956, He Taught Me Lies
3/23/02 – FREEK
3/24/02 – True Love Always + Lost Weekend, Weird Paul's "Billy Joel Loves Cakes"
3/27/02 – X27, Modey Lemon, Pay Toilets
3/28/02 – Crimson Sweet, Telstar, Philadelphia Experiment
3/30/02 – IMC Benefit w/ Sadaharu, Monster Though It Be, The Ezekial, Crowded Tombs
3/31/02 – Flying Luttenbachers, Pink and Brown, Microawaves, Manherringbone
4/1/02 – Otophobia, Crowded Tombs, Caustic Christ
4/2/02 – Two Man Advantage
4/3/02 – Sic Bay, Vaz, Pikadori, Conelrad
4/4/02 – No info for show
4/5/02 – No info for show
4/6/02 – Salt The Earth, Forward Motion, Better Off Dead
4/8/02 – Caustic Christ, Submachine, Reason of Insanity

4/13/02 – Benefit for Greater Pittsburgh Women's Shelter: Teddy Duchamp's Army, The Ezekial, Whatever it Takes, Tabula Rasa, Pikadori
4/14/02 – Detachment Kit, Owens Ring, The Spacepimps, Life In Bed
4/17/02 – Poetry reading
4/18/02 – Rocking Horse Winner, Strangers As Heroes, Forward Motion, Tabula Rasa
4/19/02 – No info for show
4/20/02 – The Code, Thought Riot
4/21/02 – Kill Devil Hills, The Ezekial, He Taught Me Lies
4/22/02 – No info for show
5/2/02 – The Copyrights, Miroslav, Extended Family, Chux Beta
5/4/02 – Midnight Scenario
5/6/02 – Small Brown Bike, Teddy Duchamp's Army
5/7/02 – Io (CD release), He Taught Me Lies, Pikadori, The Ezekial
5/8/02 – Thrones, Orthrelm, Zombi, Crucial Unit
5/10/02 – Amdi Petersens Arme, The Index, Diallo, Behind Enemy Lines, Caustic Christ, Intense Youth
5/11/02 – Warren Commission
5/17/02 – Palestine and Israel Teach in. Music by Lorelei.
5/19/02 – No info for show
5/25/02 – Gunspiking (last show), The Accident, Neotrope
5/26/02 – An Albatross
5/28/02 – He Taught Me Lies (CD release), Intense Youth, Puppy vs Dyslexia, The Meanagers
5/30/02 – Rocket 350, Sixer, The Philadelphia, Experiment, Counteraction, The Code
6/5/02 – Pg. 99
6/6/02 – Storm the Tower
6/7/02 – Book Em Benefit
6/8/02 – The Great Clearing Off, The Sound of Failure, Krooked Grind
6/10/02 – No info for show
6/12/02 – Anodyne
6/14/02 – He Taught Me Lies, Virginia Black Lung, Pikadori, The Breather Resistance
6/15/02 – No info for show
6/18/02 – Pleasure Forever
6/19/02 – The Slagheaps are Sprouting zine/art show
6/20/02 – National Blue
6/21/02 – Crucial Unit, Municipal Waste, Caustic Christ, Aphasia
6/23/02 – ETA, Def Choice, Submachine, Caustic Christ
6/24/02 – As Friends Rust
6/26/02 – Artimus Pyle
6/27/02 – Crowded Tombs, Late Night Desperate, 1905, Modey Lemon, Pikadori.
6/28/02 – This Bike is a Pipe Bomb
7/1/02 – Divit
7/3/02 – Wind Up Bird
7/5/02 – Unsound, Krooked Grind, Rich Mackin, Rosie Street Pixie
7/6/02 – FREEK
7/7/02 – Blood Brothers, Cancer Conspiracy, An Albatross, Farewell Euclid
7/8/02 – The Body, Anton Bordman, Facedowninshit, Io, The Moment
7/9/02 – Creation is Crucifixion, Crowded Tombs
7/10/02 – Glasseater
7/11/02 – Hellnation, Brody's Militia, Crucial Unit, Voetsek
7/12/02 – Gunmoll, The Attention, Corpus Cristi, Killing the Messenger, Tabula Rasa
7/13/02– IMC benefit w/ Io, He Taught Me Lies, The Accident, Stilyagi
7/15/02 – Rocking Horse Winner
7/15/02– The Rites, Cut the Shit, Caustic Christ, Corpse Grenade
7/16/02 – Paul Lynde 451
7/17/02 – DFA
7/18/02 – Daughters
7/19/02 – The Kants, Day after Yesterday, Farewell Euclid, Stilyagi
7/20/02 – Stuck in Standby
7/22/02 – Scene Creamers
7/25/02 – LIZA-Palooza!: Hiretsukan, Turnaround Norman, Step Forward Look West, Intense Youth!, Forward Motion, Stilyagi
7/26/02 – Brad Yoder
7/31/02 – Anathallo
8/1/02 – No info for show
8/2/02 – Think I Care
8/3/02 – Anah Aevia
8/4/02 – Poetry Reading
8/7/02 – No info for show
8/8/02 – The Moment, Geography, The Scent of Human History, He Taught Me Lies
8/9/02 – The Awakening, K-10 Prospect, Intense Youth, Krooked Grind
8/10/02 – Free Barrabas, The Lovehandles, Indian on a Horse, Stilyagi, Crowded Tombs
8/12/02 – Miroslav
8/12/02 – Crucial Unit, Brody's Militia, Voetsek, Damage Deposit, Divorce
8/15 /02– No info for show
8/16/02 – X27, The Weather Channel, Conelrad
8/17/02 – Dead Letter Auction
8/18/02 – No info for show
8/20/02 – Black Cat Music
8/21/02 – Backstabbers, Inc, Face Death

8/22/02 – ARA Benefit w/ Behind Enemy Lines, Death of Every Season
8/23/02 – No info for show
8/24/02 – No info for show
8/26/02 – Witch Hunt
8/29/02 – Caustic Christ
9/1/02 – No info for show
9/4/02 – He Taught Me Lies, Alpha Control Group C, Stilyagi
9/5/02 – Lorelei
9/6/02 – Yage, Io, Intense Youth, Tabula Rasa
9/8/02 – Punx Picnic
9/13/02 – No info for show
9/14/02 – Sadaharu
9/17/02 – Party of Helicopters
9/19/02 – Guitar! Guitar! Guitar! Guitar!
9/20/02 – The Copyrights, Miroslav, Planet of the Planets, Wynkataung Monks, The Merit Badges
9/21/02 – Tear It Up, Crucial Unit, Aphasia, Face Death
9/23/02 – Teen Cthulu, McVeigh, Conelrad, Io
9/28/02 – Charlevoix
9/30/02 – No info for show
10/1/02 – Cerberus Shoal, Shy Child, Requiem
10/2/02 – No Time Left
10/4/02 – No info for show
10/5/02 – Totally Awesome Dudes, Unsound
10/7/02 – Crimson Sweet, The Copyrights, Corpus Christie, Destinos
10/8/02 – No info for show
10/11/02 – Coup Fourre
10/12/02 – No info for show
10/15/02 – Voices in the Wilderness benefit w/ He Taught Me Lies, Pikadori, Intense Youth
10/17/02– Weaving the Deathbag, Aphasia, Frozen Throne
10/19/02 – No info for show
10/22/02 – No info for show
10/23/02 – Mirah, Shemo, The Accident
10/24/02 – Liar's Academy, Le Sonique, Owensring, The Reputation
10/25/02 – Explosions in the Sky, Kilowatthours, Arco Flute Foundation, All the Quiet
10/26/02 – No info for show
10/30/02 – Minus The Bear, Tabula Rasa, Snowden's Secret, The Walnut Street Project
10/31/02 – Pikadori, Neotrope, Aphasia, Krooked Grind
11/1/02 – Darkest Hour, Majority Rule, Totally Awesome Dudes, Io
11/02/02 – McVeigh, Free Barrabas, Phallic Impalement
11/4/02 – Flying Luttenbachers, Creta Bourzia, Adams and the Blackout

11/6/02 – Caustic Christ, Corpus Christie, Aphasia, Truckgrind Your Face, Suburban Death Machine
11/8/02 – ADD Fest V
11/9/02 – Trunk of Dead Bodies, The Minus Tide, Nightmare Scenario, Noticing The Mistake
11/11/02 – Free Barrabas, Robot Has Werewolf Hand, Elad Affair, Face Death
11/12/02 – Appleseed Cast, Dave Singer + the Science, The Damn Personals, The Paperchase
11/13/02 – Trial By Fire
11/15/02 – Tragedy, Behind Enemy Lines, Corpus Christie, Aphasia
11/18/02 – Marichal, Io, Murder in the Red Barn, The Channel
11/21/02 – Selfish, Caustic Christ, Krooked Grind, Intense Youth
11/22/02 – Black Rose Diary, Killing the Messenger, Last Saving Grace, Destinos, Benchwarmer
11/23/02 – No info for show
11/25/02 – Jim Munroe/Joe Meno book/zine readings
11/30/02 – Behind Enemy Lines, He Taught Me Lies, Neotrope, Aphasia
12/2/02 – Fuerza X, Crucial Unit, Conelrad, Suburban Death Machine
12/6/02 – Broken Free, Noticing The Mistake, The Caulfield Principle, Destinos
12/7/02 – No info for show
12/10/02 – Eyesores, The Rogers Sisters, The Fife The Forth, Weird Paul
12/12/02 – Against Me!, Grabass Charlestons, Army of Ponch, Black Rose Diary, Counteraction
12/13/02 – Rats Into Robots, Io, Funeral for Rosewater
12/17/02 – Clutter, Stoic Sex Pro, Unfinished Symphonies
12/18/02 – Mae
12/19/02 – No Time Left, Robot Has Werewolf Hand
12/20/02 – Caustic Christmas w/ Krooked Grind, Weekend Warriors, The Traditionals, Corpus Christie, Forward Motion, Destinos, The Indifference
12/21/02 – The Copyrights, An Offhand Way, Green is Mean, Run for India

2003

1/3/03 – Dutchland Diesel
1/4/03 – The Dead Hate the Living, Crucial Unit, At Home Rocket Booster, Insurgence, Look Alive, Caustic Christ, Annihilation Time, Suburban Death Machine
1/14/03 – Sashimi, Neotrope, Lorelei
1/16/03 – Turnaround Norman, Krooked Grind, Intense Youth, Stilyagi
1/17/03 – The Pine, Blue Hour, Marichal, Stilyagi
1/18/03 – Don Austin, The Rites, Sofa King Killer, Suburban Death Machine
1/25/03 – ARA Benefit w/ The Revolvers, Olympus Mons

1/28/03 – My Hotel Year, Believe in Toledo, Forward Motion, Run for India, Le Sonique
1/31/03 – Better Off Dead
2/4/03 – Madcap
2/6/03 – No info for show
2/7/03 – No info for show
2/8/03 – Blood Brothers, VAUX, True North, Crowded Tombs, Farewell Euclid
2/14/03 – Neptune, CNVRSNS, Adams and the Blackout, Stilyagi
2/15/03 – Rich Mackin, Hot Cross, The Fiction, Io, Mike Bolam Heavy Metal Spoken Word
2/25/03 – Ten Grand, Grand Ulena, Conelrad
2/27/03 – breaking pangea
2/28/03 – No info for show
3/1/03 – The Revolvers, The Ransoms, Counteraction, Black Rose Diary, Unsound
3/3/03 – Chase Theory, Tabula Rasa
3/5/03 – The One AM Radio, The Wind Up Bird, Marichal, Hey Sky
3/7/03 – Calvary, Yaphet Kotto, Pikadori, Io
3/8/03 – No info for show
3/11/03 – Light the Fuse and Run, Advocate, Free Barabbas, Geography
3/14/03 – Forward Motion, Members of the Yellow Press, New Grenada, The Clampdown, The Trembling
3/15/03 – Divorce, Crucial Unit, The Sound of Failure, Race To Die, Intense Youth
3/18/03 – Eufio, The Accident, Films by Valie Export and Vera Chytilova
3/19/03 – Frostiva, Lorelei, The Copyrights, Benchwarmer, Destinos
3/20/03 – Municipal Waste, Crucial Unit, Caustic Christ, Project Grizzly, Herod
3/21/03 – No info for show
3/22/03 – The Cinema Eye, The Minus Tide, Audion
3/24/03 – Dead Hate The Living
3/25/03 – Shade, Collapse
3/26/03 – No info for show
3/27/03 – Allergic to Whores, Krooked Grind, Aphasia, Inverted
3/28/03 – Ampline
3/29/03 – Teddy Duchamp's Army (final show), The Code, Whatever It Takes, Crucial Unit, Creta Bourzia
4/1/03 – Akimbo, Free Barabbas, McVeigh, Ghostpoppers
4/3/03 – A–set, The Channel, Economist, Life in Bed
4/5/03 – Plan A Project
4/7/03 – Kinski, Missing Pilots , Marichal, Aydin
4/8/03 – Minus the Bear, Life In Bed, Tabula Rasa
4/9/03 – Caustic Christ, Corpus Christie, Intense Youth, Suburban Death Machine
4/10/03 – The Moment
4/11/03 – No info for show
4/12/03 – No info for show
4/14/03 – Lucero, The Copyrights, Augie Leonard Sr.
4/15/03 – Discharge Information System, Behind Enemy Lines, Aphasia, Pain Dogs
4/16/03 – Ghostpoppers, Summers Dying, Free Barrabas, The Squints, Methal Orange
4/17/03 – Leprosy, Aphelion, Velvet Hollow
4/18/03 – Girlish Figure, Chromolodeon, Counteraction, Better Off Dead, Krooked Grind
4/19/03 – Caustic Christ, RAMBO, Crucial Unit, Krooked Grind
4/21/03 – Drop Science, Adams and the Blackout, The Silver Thread, The Channel
4/23/03 – Crimson Sweet, The Copyrights, Sixtyfour
4/25/03 – David Is Burning
4/26/03 – The Motion, Del Cielo, Sleep Station, The Accident, Curses and Kisses
4/30/03 – The Apes, Lorelei, Farewell Euclid, New Alcindors
5/2/03 – West Coast of the East Coast release show w/ Lorelei, Pay Toilets, The Copyrights, The Human Brains, Aphasia, Adams and The Blackout
5/3/03 – Behind Enemy Lines, Aphasia, Krooked Grind, Waiting Could Crush
5/7/03 – No info for show
5/8/03 – Blacken the Skies
5/9/03 – Valkyrie, Silencio, The Caterpillar Scheme, The Affair
5/10/03 – No info for show
5/12/03 – Mono, A Frames, The Copyrights
5/15/03 – Fiya, The Channel
5/16/03 – IMC benefit w/ Io, Facedowninshit, Kylesa, Aphasia, Intense Youth!
5/20/03 – A Global Threat
5/22/03 – Murder In The Red Barn, The Copyrights, The Barrett Black Band
5/24/03 – Bazhena, Aim of Conrad, Christiansen, Aphasia, The Affair
5/29/03 – Guyana Punchline, Crucial Unit, 70,000 BC, Conelrad
5/30/03 – GC5
6/2/03 – Trunk Full of Dead Bodies, A Choir Invisible, Master Mechanic
6/3/03 – Hawnay Troof, Dead By Dawn, Resurrectum
6/4/03 – The South, Operation: Latte Thunder, Io, Its a Fuckin Trap, Free Barrabas
6/5/03 – K-10 Prospect, Carrie Nations, Krooked Grind, Kiamo Ko
6/6/03 – IAN FEST: Crucial Unit, Behind Enemy Lines, Born/Dead, Deadfall, Intense Youth!, Phalanx

6/7/03 – Holding On, Modern Life Is War, Farewell Hope, xLooking Forwardx, Drain This Blood, Waiting the Storm
6/10/03 – Food Not Bombs benefit w/ Krooked Grind, The Indifference, Sammaharas Betrayal, Forward Motion
6/13/03 – Anarchaos, Blasting Caps, Bunny Five Coat
6/14/03 – Aphasia, Crucial Unit, Caustic Christ, Behind Enemy Lines, Krooked Grind, Bastard Sons of Colonel Crawford
6/16/03 – 1905, Tradition Dies Here, Krooked Grind
6/17/03 – From A Second Story Window, Liegia, Broken Free, Drain This Blood, Aversion Therapy
6/19/03 – The Sainte Catherines, Favorite Atomic Hero, Rescue, Anarchaos
6/21/03 – Hypatia, Robot Attack, Wolves, Donna and Carly, Intense Youth
6/23/03 – True North, Black Cross, Point of Attack, Halo Perfecto, He Taught Me Lies
6/24/03 – Forever Means Goodbye
6/25/03 – From Ashes Rise, Assault, Kamikaze, Fanshen, Caustic Christ, Krooked Grind
6/27/03 – The French Connection, How to Beat A Dead Horse
6/28/03 – Reason of Insanity, Pretty Little Flowers, Deathly Fighter, Case of Emergency, Caustic Christ
7/1/03 – Antelope
7/3/03 – Dear Diary I Seem to be Dead
7/5/03 – No info for show
7/7/03 – Floor
7/12/03 – No info for show
7/15/03 – Tear It Up, The Rites, Cut The Shit, Caustic Christ, Corpse Grenade
7/16/03 – Anita Fix
7/17/03 – Light the Fuse and Run, Transistor Transistor, Ass-end Offend, Forward Motion .
7/18/03 – Hot Cross
7/19/03 – Embrace Today, Cast Aside, Waiting the Storm, Drain This Blood
7/21/03 – Since by Man, Cursed, A Life Once Lost, Crowded Tombs, Forward Motion
7/24/03 – An Albatross
7/25/03 – Broken, Blue Rose Liar, Behind Enemy Lines, Aphasia
7/26/03 – A Petal Fallen
7/29/03 – Wormwood, Hewhocorrupts, Dark Magus, Spliff aka Wheels of Contusion
8/1/03 – No info for show
8/2/03 – Crucial Unit, Aphasia, Caustic Christ, Pay Toilets, DFA
8/4/03 – Members of the Yellow Press, Kakistocracy, The Last Will Be The First, Sequoia
8/5/03 – Wake Up On Fire, Contravene, Magrudergrind

8/6/03 – Blame Game, Zann, Krooked Grind, He Taught Me Lies
8/8/03 – Pipedown, Whatever It Takes, The Codes, Tabular Rasa
8/9/03 – J Church
8/12/03 – Crucial Unit, Divorce
8/13/03 – Del Cielo, Shoutbus, Alpha Control Group C, Aydin, Thousandaire
8/14/03 – Too Pure To Die, Love's Despair, Orange Alert, Waiting The Storm, Go It Alone, Drain This Blood, End Your Life
8/15/03 – Ampere, They and the Children, The Sidewalk Berserkers, Face Death
8/18/03 – Thumbs Up, Living Under Lies, Conelrad
8/19/03 – Robot Has Werewolf Hand, They Live, Ice Capades
8/21/03 – Zine reading and Chili cookoff
8/22/03 – The Clancey Six, Krooked Grind, Turn Around Norman, Free Barrabas, Mischief Brew
8/23/03 – Sulaco, Ken Mode
8/25/03 – No info for show
8/28/03 – No info for show
9/5/03 – Sequoia, The Combine, He Taught Me Lies, Walk Through Walls
9/6/03 – Caustic Christ (LP release), Despite, Behind Enemy Lines, Intense Youth, Suburban Death Machine
9/7/03 – Punx Picnic
9/9/03 – Cold Sides, The Nein, The Channel
9/10/03 – No info for show
9/11/03 – No info for show
9/13/03 – Vale and Year, Between the Devil and the Deep Blue Sea, Bazhena, Redshift
9/17/03 – No info for show
9/18/03 – The Spark, Stop It!, Ice Capades, Suburban Death Machine
9/19/03 – Hellnation, Krooked Grind, Quill
9/20/03 – Submission Hold, 1905, The Chase, The Moment, Fear is the Mindkiller
9/26/03 – No info for show
9/29/03 – Municipal Waste, Caustic Christ, Bread and Water, Guarda, Suburban Death Machine
10/2/03 – No info for show
10/3/03 – Vena Cava, The Everyothers, Ice Capades, Harangue
10/4/04 – Hooray for Everything
10/6/03 – Born Dead Icons, La Fraction, Aphasia, Suburban Death Machine
10/7/03 – Akimbo, Swing By Seven, Ice Capades, Sequoia
10/13/03 – Paint it Black, Voice in the Wire, Adam Social, Ice Capades, Point of Attack
10/14/03 – Movement Three, Mary Celeste, He Taught Me Lies
10/20/03 – Phantom Limbs, Pay Toilets, Caustic Christ, Conelrad
10/21/03 – Oil

10/22/03 – Kissing Tigers, Bobby Birdman, YACHT
10/23/03 – Vegan Bake off
10/24/03 – Where It Ends, Too Pure To Die, Drain This Blood, Armed Battery
10/25/03 – Conelrad, Mary Celeste, Vale and Year
10/31/03 – Born Dead Icons
11/1/03 – Okkervil River, Harangue, Vale and Year
11/4/03 – Del Rey, Arrivals and Departures, Lorelei
11/6/03 – Discharge Information System, Another Dying Democracy, The Wives, Behind Enemy Lines
11/7/03 – ADD Fest VI : Behind Enemy Lines, Conelrad, He Taught Me Lies, Mary Celeste, Point of Attack, Vale and Year, Arrivals and Departures, Curses and Kisses, Ice Capades, Sequoia
11/8/03 – Wrangler Brutes, Off Minor, To the Mean, Adams and the Blackout, Triangle and Rhino
11/10/03– Desert City Soundtrack, Tabula Rasa
11/14/03 – The Gunshy
11/15/03 – Notes on Rainier
11/17/03 – Defiance Ohio, Eliza Furnace, The AK47's, Madeline, Dinasaurs Baseball and Hopscotch
11/18/03 – Watch Them Die
11/20/03 – No Time Left, Abusing the Word, From Ashes Rise, Krooked Grind
11/22/03 – Burning Star Core, Mike Shiflter
11/25/03 – Resolve, Caustic Christ, Aphasia
11/29/03 – I Farm
12/4/03 – Arms Bend Back
12/5/03 – Behind Enemy Lines (CD release show), The Total End, Caustic Christ, Aphasia, Krooked Grind
12/11/03 – Sweetheart, Between the Devil and the Deep Blue Sea, Ice Capades, Curses and Kisses
12/12/03 – Suffer The Fate, Armed Battery, End of Humanity, End Your Life
12/16/03 – The Black Dahlia Murder, Three Inches of Blood, Himsa, The Caulfield Principle, Suffer The Fat
12/19/03 – Threatener, Caustic Christ, Direct Control, Krooked Grind, Suburban Death Machine
12/23/03 – No info for show
12/29/03 – The Fiction, Mary Celeste, Sequoia, Adam Social
12/30/03 – Running For Cover, Project Grizzly, Eat Shit And Die, Adam Social

2004

1/2/04 – On the Rise, Armed Battery, Drain This Blood, Suffer The Fate, Another Way, Endsfall
1/3/04 – No info for show
1/4/04–Annihilation Time, Caustic Christ, Mantooth and Ovens' Return Show
1/7/04 –No info for show
1/8/04 – The Spark, FLAK, Look Back and Laugh
1/9/04 – Roboto Benefit w/ Voice In the Wire, The Ruin, Sun Tornado, The Setup
1/10/04 – The Forms, Mary Celeste, Ice Capades, Life In Bed
1/11/04 – The Body, Late Night Prayers, He Taught Me Lies, Slices
1/24/04 – True If Destroyed, Curses and Kisses, Aydin
1/29/04 – The Insides, The Dammit Janets, The Moment, A Beautiful Mess
1/30/04 – This Bike Is A Pipebomb, Evil Robot Us, City Hands aka Zack Furness, Adam Social
1/31/04 – No info for show
2/4/04– Icons of Filth, Thought Crime, Behind Enemy Lines, Krooked Grind
2/5/04 – No info for show
2/7/04 – No info for show
2/10/04 – Sex Worker Art Show
2/13/04 – Benefit for the Big Idea w/ Boombox, Mary Celeste, Ice Capades, Redshift
2/14/04 – No info for show
2/17/04 – Spaghetti Social w/ Styles For Modern Living, Levitate
2/20/04 – Aphasia (7" release)
2/21/04 – 25 Ta Life, Not Without Resistance, Deliberate Intent, End Your Life
2/22/04 – *Afropunk* video showing
2/28/04 – Clamor Magazine Anniversary Party w/ Rick Gribenas, Styles For Modern Living, Requiem, Turn Around Norman, He Taught Me Lies
3/6/04 – No info for show
3/12/04 – Beneath the Ashes
3/13/04 – A Day in Black and White
3/15/04 – No info for show
3/16/04 – Spaghetti Social w/ Deadly Swarms of Dangerous Bees, RelativeQ
3/19/04 – No info for show
3/20/04 – Cast Aside, Derringer, End Your Life
3/21/04 – Vitamin X, Fourteen or Fight, Punch in the Face, Fucked Up, No Time Left
3/26/04 – Hiretsukan, Marathon, Sun Tornado, Sequoia
3/27/04 – No info for show
3/29/04 – No info for show
4/2/04 – Conelrad (7" release), Suburban Death Machine, Aphasia, Loose Nut (Caustic Christ as Black Flag), Iced Tea Is The Bastard (Crucial Unit as Man is the Bastard)

4/3/04 – No info for show
4/4/04 – Cat on Form, Off Minor, Sequioa, Tabula Rasa
4/8/04 – Cursed
4/9/04 – J Church, The Methadones, Suburban Death Machine, Hit Me Back
4/10/04 – Defiance, Ohio, City Hands/Zack Furness, Hissyfit
4/12/04 – Navies, He Taught Me Lies, The Gunshy
4/17/04 – Brass Castle, Ice Capades, Assfaxxxx
4/22/04 – Summer Dying
4/23/04 – Yaphet Kotto, Mannequin, He Taught Me Lies with Rick Gribenas, Allies, The sea, like lead
4/25/04 – No info for show
4/30/04 – No info for show
5/4/04 – No info for show
5/7/04 – Mach Tiver, The Narrows, Ice Capades, Southpaw
5/8/04 – Fighting Dogs, Allies, He Taught Me Lies with Rick Gribenas, Dismal
5/10/04 – No info for show
5/14/04 – No info for show
5/15/04 – Western PA Fund For Choice Benefit w/ Jim Steiner, Allies, He Taught Me Lies with Rick Gribenas, Crucial Unit
5/17/04 – Runnamucks , Caustic Christ, Krooked Grind
5/21/04 – Aydin, Allies, He Taught Me Lies with Rick Gribenas, Styles For Modern Living
5/22/04 – USAISAMONSTER, Sun Tornado, Meetthebutcher, Slices, Wrestling Team
5/25/04 – No info for show
5/27/04 – Pretty Faces, Dance Dance El Captain, Sequoia, Mary Celeste
5/28/04 – Case of Emergency, Prurient, Air Conditioning, Pissed Jeans, Adam Social
5/29/04 – Crowd Deterrent, Totally Awesome Dudes, Drain this Blood, Adam Social
6/2/04 – Stop It
6/3/04 – He Taught Me Lies with Rick Gribenas, Movement Three, Conelrad
6/4/04 – Emphasis, the sea, like lead, Meetthebutcher, A is A, Slices
6/5/04 – Department of Homeland Security, Adam Social, Wheels of Confusion aka Spliff, Warzone Womyn
6/7/04 – Tyranny of Shaw, Anchorage, Corpse Grenade, Warzone Womyn
6/10/04 – Answer Lies
6/11/04 No info for show
6/12/04 – Keep Laughing
6/15/04 – Artimus Pyle, Sunday Morning Einsteins, Fuckedupmess, FLAK, Caustic Christ
6/17/04 – Amanda Woodward

6/18/04 – The Spark
6/19/04 – Bailout
6/20/04 – Forward
6/21/04 – Forca Macabre
6/22/04 – 1905, bread and roses
6/24/04 – Bury the Living
6/25/04 – xLooking Forwardx, 10-33, CDC
6/26/04 – The Great Clearing Off
6/28/04 – No info for show
6/29/04 – Turn Around Norman, He Taught Me Lies with Rick Gribenas, Fuckedupmess, End Me
7/1/04 – Too Pure To Die, XSuffocate FasterX, Nehemiah, XKill EveryoneX, Suffer The Fate
7/2/04 – Sleeper Cell
7/3/04 – Tiny Hawks, the sea, like lead, Allies
7/5/04 – Hudson Falcons
7/7/04 – The Profits
7/8/04 – The Syndicate, He Taught Me Lies with Rick Gribenas, La-Z-Boyz, A Is A
7/9/04 – Mischief Brew, Evil Robot Us, City Hands/Zack Furness
7/10/04 – No info for show
7/13/04 – This Ship Will Sink, Kodan Armada, Southpaw, Anchorage
7/14/04 – Tropieza
7/16/04 – Direct Control, Kabuki Thunder, Suburban Death Machine
7/18/04 – Scurvy Dawgs, Hue and Cry, Stilyagi
7/21/04 – No info for show
7/23/04 – Uzi Suicide, Hollowed Out, Fuckedupmess
7/26/04 – Donnybrook, Sex Positions, Not Without Resistance, Bottom Line, At Hopes End
7/28/04 – Mykado
7/30/04 – Del Cielo, Allies, He Taught Me Lies
7/31/04 – Ampere, the sea, like lead, Wake Up On Fire, Krooked Grind
8/2/04 – Athletic Automaton, Sun Tornado, Edie Sedgewick, Slices, Mary Celeste
8/3/04 – Bruce Banner, Deadfall, STFU, Strung Up, Caustic Christ
8/4/04 – Don Austin
8/7/04 – No info for show
8/10/04 – No info for show
8/14/04 – Soophie Nun Squad, Defiance, Ohio, McGonigle
8/18/04 – Planes Mistaken for Stars, Voice In The Wire
8/20/04 – Vivisick
8/21/04 – The Dead Hate the Living, Witch Hunt, Skeletal Witch
8/24/04 – Victims
8/26/04 – Sinaloa, Arrivals and Departures, Aydin

8/27/04 – The Sound of Failure, He Taught Me Lies
8/28/04 – Treason
9/2/04 – Die Young
9/3/04 – Western PA Fund for Choice benefit
9/4/04 – Cold Sweat, True If Destroyed, Suburban Death Machine, Warzone Womyn
9/7/04 – Weather, Adams and the Blackout, Slices
9/9/04 – Doomsday 99, Ice Capades
9/11/04 – The Grand Collision, Life at These Speeds
9/15/04 – No info for show
9/16/04 – No info for show
9/17/04 – No info for show
9/18/04 – Voice in the Wire (CD release), Origin, Creta Bourzia, The Code
9/20/04 – Hulk Smash
9/23/04 – Skitsystem
9/25/04 – Fucked Up, Career Suicide, Caustic Christ, Suburban Death Machine
10/9/04 – Record swap
10/12/04 – No!
10/13/04 – Voice In The Wire, Paint It Black
10/14/04 – Signal Lost, Caustic Christ
10/22/04 – Kathy Kashel
10/23/04 – Caustic Christ, Municipal Waste, Crucial Unit
10/27/04 – Uncurbed, Hero Dishonest, Star Strangled Bastard, Suburban Death Machine
10/28/04 – Wrangler Brutes, Takaru, Ice Capades, Two Sexy Beasts
10/29/04 – Rooftop Films video showing
10/30/04 – Microcosm video showing + zine reading
11/1/04 – Endless Nightmare
11/3/04 – No info for show
11/4/04 – The Advantage
11/5/04 – Human Brains
11/10/04 – Moore Brothers
11/12/04 – ADD Fest VII: A is A, Aydin, Fangs of the Panda, Fuckedupmess, FLAK, Origen aka Will Stanton, the sea, like lead, Slice Capades with Teen Mushroom, Southpaw, Warzone Womyn
11/20/04 – World Burns to Death, Kegcharge, Caustic Christ, Suburban Death Machine
11/27/04 – Del Cielo, Vale and Year, A Is A, Zach Curl
12/3/04 – Warzone Womyn, Brainhandle, FLAK
12/4/04– Death Before Dishonour, Suffer the Fate, Lionheart, The Pledge
12/12/04 – Cattle Decapitation, Conelrad, Corpse Grenade
12/29/04 – Department of Homeland Security (didn't play), FLAK, Snowjob

2005

1/5/05 – The Spark, Ruiner
1/9/05 – Backstabbers Inc
1/11/05 – The Body, Late Night Prayers, He Taught Me Lies, Slices with Bradam Streiple
1/12/05 – Yowie, Conelrad, Pay Toilets
1/14/05 – Modey Lemon, Two Sexy Beasts, Wizardfight
1/15/05 – Voice In The Wire, Marathon, the sea, like lead, Fue de Joie
1/24/05 – Forward To Death
1/31/05 – StillxIII
2/1/05 – An Albatross, Pay Toilets
2/4/05 – Tumor Feast
2/10/05 – From This Day On, Demise of Eros, Today Is The Grave, Too Pure To Die
2/15/05 – Static Age, Mommy and Daddy, Eyes Like Knives, Southpaw
2/17/05 – The Spunks, The Radio Beats, Kim Phuc
2/19/05 – Tommy Gutless, Two Bit Hoods, Outclassed
2/25/05 – Zegota, 1905, Pain Dogs, Sinners in the Hands of an Angry God
2/26/05 – RAMBO, Caustic Christ, Municipal Waste, Asshole Parade, Warzone Womyn
3/5/05 – Del Cielo, Des Ark, Allies, Fangs of the Panda
3/11/05 – Voice In The Wire, Signal Home, He Taught Me Lies, The Loved Ones
3/12/05 – Oxford Collapse, the sea, like lead, Southpaw
3/14/05 – Since the Flood
3/19/05 – Cardiac Arrest, Brain Handle, End Me, Happy News Please, Dead Operator
3/22/05 – Riisteyt, To What End?, Die Screaming, FLAK
3/23/05 – Blacklisted, Dead Hearts, Today is the Grave, Lionheart, Van Dammage
3/24/05 – The Spark, AutoDixx
3/25/05 – Hulk Smash, Slices, Warzone Womyn, Young Men's Department
3/27/05 – Fighting Dogs, Stations, Warzone Womyn, Shitdogs of War
3/28/05 – Improv Night
3/29/05 – World Festival of Youth benefit
4/1/05 – Suburban Death Machine, Caustic Christ, FLAK, Kim Phuc
4/2/05 – Western PA Fund for Choice benefit w/ He Taught Me Lies, In Violet, Behind Enemy Lines, The Motorpsychos
4/4/05 – Bellafea, Company Anthem, End Me, Mikey C and Tom
4/7/05 – Toys That Kill, Radio Beats, Brainhandle
4/9/05 – Stockyard Stoics, The Ware Is On, Speak Out!
4/12/05 – The Body, the sea, like lead, Sequoia

4/13/05 – Funeral Diner, AutoDixx, Sinners in the Hands of an Angry God
4/14/05 – Emperor X, Ice Capades, Zach Curl, Rote Kapelle
4/16/05 – Edfest featuring Fucked Up, Career Suicide, Violent Minds, Wound Up, Brainhandle, Caustic Christ
4/18/05 – Kylesa, Kim Phuc, Fuckedupmess, Die Screaming
4/19/05 – Defiance Ohio, Sequoia, Zack Furness, Mahi Mahi, Smut
4/23/05 – Belegost, Allies, the sea, like lead, Vale and Year
4/24/05 – Fifth Hour Hero, Tabula Rasa, Kudzu Wish, The OPD
4/27/05 – The Explosion, Throw Rag, The Loved Ones, Voice In The Wire
4/28/05 – Born/Dead, Behind Enemy Lines, FLAK, Dawn of Ruin
4/30/05 – Annihilation Time, Caustic Christ, Warzone Womyn, Slices
5/1/05 – Tranny Roadshow
5/3/05 – "Long Run of Small Steps" compilation release: He Taught Me Lies, Vale and Year, the sea, like lead, Fuckedupmess, Two Sexy Beasts
5/6/05 – Endless Fight
5/12/05 – Immortal Avenger, The Infection, Lethal Infection, Oh Shit They're Going to Kill Us, Magic Wolf
5/14/05 – Gunspiking, Fear is the Mindkiller, Nux Vomica, D2K, Zack Furness
5/18/05 – Giant Haystacks, Fuckedupmess, Suburban Death Machine, Kim Phuc
5/19/05 – Akimbo, Conifer, Ice Capades
5/21/05 – What secrets?, Droopy Septum/Tusk Lord, Adams and the Blackout, Mikey C and Tom
5/26/05 – Bodies Lay Broken, Rotten Sound, Misery Index, Magrudergrind, Spoonful of Vicodin
5/27/05 – A Is A, Red Knife Lottery, Arms Over Arteries
5/28/05 – World Festival of Youth benefit
5/31/05 – VCR, Creta Bourzia, Valiant Thorr
6/1/05 – Burial Year, Sinners in the Hands of an Angry God
6/4/05 – The Fucks, Moneymadridmadagascar, The Neverminds
6/6/05 – Housequake, Pimps Up Ho-down, Fear Is the Mindkiller, Allies, MC Homeless
6/8/05 – The Teeth, Greg Cislon Ensemble, Developer, Ladies Beware of an Architect, Luxe-Robotica
6/9/05 – Unpersons, Adams and the Blackout, Young Men's Department
6/10/05 – Iron Lung, Running for Cover, Warzone Womyn, Fuckedupmess
6/15/05 – Selfish, Hellshock, Behind Enemy Lines, No Fucker, FLAK
6/17/05 – World Festival of Youth Benefit
6/18/05 – The State, Caustic Christ, Brain Handle
6/19/05 – Buried Inside
6/20/05 – Chromolodeon
6/21/05 – Bullets In, Sea Creatures, Ice Capades, Sequoia
6/22/05 – Bayonettes
6/23/05 – World Downfall
6/26/05 – Municipal Waste, Coliseum, Caustic Christ, I Object
6/27/05 – World Festival of Youth Benefit
6/28/05 – Blacklisted
6/29/05 – Drowningman
7/1/05 – Oxford Collapse
7/7/05 – Poser Disposer
7/8/05 – Wrong Day to Quit
7/11/05 – The Close, Goodbye Ohio, Housequake, Slingshot Dakota
7/13/05 – Seein' Red, Bury The Living, Kriegstanz, Caustic Christ, Brain Handle
7/14/05 – Fleas and Lice, Suburban Death Machine
7/16/05 – 86 Mentality
7/18/05 – Navies, Welcome the Plague Year
7/20/05 – Latterman, Karate for Kids, Zack Furness, Sequoia
7/23/05 – Hawdcoah Magic
7/24/05 – Citizen Fish, Carpenter Ant, Kim Phuc, He Taught Me Lies
7/25/05 – Baroness, Pyramid Scheme, Shit Mayor, Sequoia, Tunturi
7/28/05 – Skitkidz, Caustic Christ, Warzone Womyn, Battle of Gettysburg
7/29/05 – Nux Vomica
8/2/05 – Disconnect, Bafabegiya, The Valley Arena, Nancy Drew
8/3/05 – Aghast
8/5/05 – Erik Peterson/Mischief Brew, Evil Robot Us, Zack Furness, D2K, McGonigle
8/6/05 – Nakano, Kalon, Southpaw, the sea, like lead
8/8/05 – The Breaks, Brain Handle, Pyramid Scheme
8/9/05 – Krum Bums
8/10/05 – Kakistocracy, Countdown to Armageddon, Behind Enemy Lines, Schifosi
8/12/05 – Hiretsukan, Coliseum, Fangs of the Panda
8/13/05 – Warzone Womyn, The Endless Blockade
8/16/05 – Dropdead, Asshole Parade, Caustic Christ, FLAK
8/17/05 – Disrespect, Red Menace, Behind Enemy Lines, Diversity Without An Issue
8/20/05 – True If Destroyed, Del Cielo, He Taught Me Lies, Southpaw
8/22/05 – I Object
8/25/05 – Las Crisi
8/26/05 – Cipher
9/1/05 – Mt Gigantic
9/7/05 – The Body, the sea, like lead, Sequoia
9/10/05 – Anti-recruitment benefit
9/12/05 – MDC
9/14/05 – Blood In Blood Out
9/16/05 – Cursed

9/17/05 – Swirling Vortex of Terror zine release w/ Pay Toilets, the sea, like lead, Sequoia
9/21/05 – Sprouts
9/22/05 – Caustic Christ (7" release), Kim Phuc, Warzone Womyn, Brain Handle
9/29/05 – Pound for Pound
9/30/05 – Minsk
10/5/05 – Hudson Falcons
10/11/05 – Made In Secret video showing
10/14/05 – Spirit In the Stairway
10/15/05 – 1913 Massacre, All Good Heroes Go To Hell, The Relapse, Degradable Society
10/16/05 – 1905, Ballast, Behind Enemy Lines, Mourning After
10/17/05 – Regulations, Caustic Christ, Suburban Death Machine
10/21/05 – Formaldehyde Junkies, Black SS, Raining Bricks, Brain Handle, Sewercide
10/22/05 – Shiver, Tommy Gutless, The Balcony Boys, Unarmed
10/26/05 – Curses and Kisses, Ice Capades, the sea, like lead, Poison Arrow
10/27/05 – Shit Mayor, Young Men's Department, Fangs of the Panda, Harangue, He Taught Me Lies
10/28/05 – FLAK (record release show), Brain Handle, Trauma, Incoming Fire, Fuckedupmess
11/1/05 – Kylesa, Coliseum, Torche, the sea, like lead
11/4/05 – Facedowninshit, Sequoia, Sinners in the Hands of an Angry God
11/7/05 – Imperial, The Hope of Change, Once Nothing, Demise of Eros
11/9/05 – Syzslak
11/11/05 – ADD Fest VIII : Magic Wolf, Microwaves, Allies, Brain Handle, Young Men's Department, Harangue, The Sexes, Mourning After, Tusk Lord Big Band
11/18/05 – the sea, like lead, Commando Kelly, He Taught Me Lies
11/19/05 – Ian Fest 4.20
11/20/05 – Suburban Death Machine, Under Pressure, Incoming Fire
11/25/05 – Sin Orden, Condenada, FLAK
11/30/05 – Reactionary Three, Smells Like Gina, He Taught Me Lies, Meetthebutcher
12/4/05 – Gouka, FLAK, Mourning After
12/10/05 – Weaving the Deathbag, Warzone Womyn, Fuckedupmess
12/13/05 – Terminal State
12/16/05 – The Ghouls, Chaotic Alliance, Nobody's Hero, Unarmed
12/17/05 – No show info
12/19/05 – The Max Levine Ensemble, Allies, Victoria Jackal, Delay
12/27/05 – Imperial Leather, Motorpsychos, Behind Enemy Lines, Officer Down
12/30/05 – Devola, Commando Kelly, Zelazowa, Vale and Year
12/31/05 – I Accuse, XBrainiaX, Warzone Womyn, Build Your Weapons

2006

1/3/06 – xBishopx
1/4/06 – Pink Razors
1/5/06 – So I Had to Shoot Him, Brown Angel
1/7/06 – Man the Conveyers, Broken, Behind Enemy Lines, Mourning After
1/10/06 – The Boils
1/12/06 – Never Surrender
1/13/06 – Grand Buffet, Dirty Faces, Poison Arrow
1/14/06 – Die Young
1/15/06 – Fighting Dogs
1/17/06 – Holy Shit!
1/19/06 – Sparrows Swarm and Sing, the sea, like lead, Kalon, He Taught Me Lies
1/21/06 – Drain This Blood
2/4/06 – the sea, like lead, Belegost, Allies, Mikey C and Tom
2/7/06 – Ghost Mice, Endless Mike and the Beagle Club, City Hands, Unarmed
2/9/06 – New Mexican Disaster Squad, Caustic Christ, Allies, Hank Jones
2/11/06 – Radio Beats (record release), Pay Toilets, Warzone Womyn
2/14/06 – Hoods
2/19/06 – Thin the Herd
2/23/06 – Buried Inside
2/24/06 – Anti-Recruitment benefit w/The Code, Unarmed, He Taught Me Lies
2/25/06 – Dirty Black Summer, Terminal State, Government Warning, FLAK
2/26/06 – The Spark
3/1/06 – Resistant Culture, Mouth Sewn Shut, Officer Down
3/3/06 – Big Idea Benefit w/ Flotilla Way, Fuckedupmess, the sea, like lead
3/5/06 – Akimbo, Rosetta, Midnite Snake, Cranes, Ice Capades
3/6/06 – Mt. Gigantic, Kickball, Lucas Sloppy's Flying Organ, Allies
3/11/06 – Sinner, Zack Curl, Pyramids, Capsule
3/18/06 – Formaldehyde Junkies, Chronic Seizure, Caustic Christ, Brain Handle
3/20/06 – Max Levine Ensemble, Boogdish, CJ's Turtle
3/21/06 – A Day In Black and White, Freedom, the sea, like lead, Massif
3/24/06 – Deadfall, I Object, Caustic Christ
3/25/06 – Pyramid Scheme (7" release), FLAK, Build Your Weapons
3/28/06 – The Wayward, Defcon 4, Allies, Student House Painters
3/30/06 – Monster Squad, Action, The Weekend Warriors, The Cheats

3/31/06 – The Drift, the sea, like lead, Natura Nasa, Lovely Ladies
4/1/06 – Municipal Waste, Baroness, Lethal Aggression, Caustic Christ, Ice Capades
4/3/06 – Toxic Holocaust, Bludwulf, Meltdown, Wrathcobra
4/8/06 – Roboto Arts Fair and Media Swap (at the Spinning Plate)
4/12/06 – A is A, Endless Mike and the Beagle Club, Elementary Thought Process, Red Knife Lottery
4/14/06 – Doomsday 1999, Warzone Womyn, Tunturi, Build Your Weapons
4/15/06 – the sea, like lead, October, Lucas Sloppy's Flying Organ, Vale and Year
4/21/06 – Slingshot Dakota, Allies, Flotilla Way, Isha and Zetta
4/22/06 – La Otracina
4/29/06 – Commando Kelly, Past Pluto, Zelazowa, Devola
5/3/06 – Clit 45, Career Soliders, Tommy Gutless, Unarmed
5/4/06 – Victims, FLAK, Wrathcobra
5/6/06 – Pedestrians, Storm The Tower, No Slogan, Brain Handle, Burial Year
5/7/06 – None More Black, Hank Jones, Unarmed, The Relapse
5/9/06 – Somerset, Southcott, Life in Bed, Sing the Evens Play the Odds
5/11/06 – Parts and Labor, Measles Mumps Rubella, Centipede E'est, Slur
5/13/06 – The Fire Still Burns, Explode and make Up, Unarmed
5/17/06 – Isha and Zetta, Magic Wolf, Harangue, Brain Handle
5/22/06 – Hem and Haw, The New Idea Society, He Taught Me Lies
5/24/06 – Blame Game, Echo Is Your Love, the sea, like lead, Poisoned Era
6/4/06 – Art Show
6/7/06 – End of a Year, Dear Tonight, Mans, Southpaw, Safety Grenade
6/9/06 – Caustic Christ, Build Your Weapons, Unreal City
6/13/06 – The Max Levine Ensemble, Canine Sugar, Chugga Chugga
6/14/06 – Magrudergrind, Tunturi, Build Your Weapons, Thrak
6/16/06 – One Be Lo
6/17/06 – The Fire Still Burns, Killed by the Bull, Explode and Make Up, Unarmed, Gasoline Dion
6/21/06 – Limpwrist, Look Back and Laugh, Unreal City
6/26/06 – Skarp, Mouth Sewn Shut, Refuse The Dirt
6/28/06 – Towers, Peter and Craig, Track of Monarchs, He Taught Me Lies
6/29/06 – The Latterman, Yo Man Go!, The Mighty Ohio, Ragweed
6/30/06 – Comadre, Graf Orlock
7/3/06 – Conversions, Capsule, Brain Handle, the sea, like lead
7/6/06 – The Rocket Arcadia, The Mark of a Moderate Man, Fuckedupmess, the sea, like lead
7/8/06 – Dancing Feet March To War, Warzone Womyn, Fighting Dogs, FLAK, Runnamucks
7/11/06 – Book 'Em Benefit w/ This Bike Is a Pipebomb, Endless Mike and the Beagle Club, City Hands
7/18/06 – Lorna Doom, Flotilla Way, Sleep Little One Sleep
7/21/06 – Bumblkaat, Alarms and Sirens, Pyramid Scheme, Blood Vessels to Wires, Refuse the Dirt
7/27/06 – Another Dying Democracy, Refuse the Dirt, Blood Vessels to Wires
8/1/06 – They and the Children, Daniel Striped Tiger, Concorida Discors, Xrinarms, Brown Angel
8/2/06 – The Summer We Went West, Hobis, He Taught Me Lies, Flotilla Way
8/3/06 – Thrak, Brain Handle, Get Rad
8/5/06 – Thin The Herd, No Fucker, FLAK, 1point3
8/6/06 – Iron Age, Bafabegiya, Both Blind, Pyramid Scheme
8/7/06 – Morgue Mart, Terror Level Red
8/12/06 – Throwing Shrapnel, The Zimmerman Note, Embludgeoned, Animal Mother
8/14/06 – This Flood Covers the Earth, Lanterns, Sleep Little One Sleep, Full Color Illustrations
8/18/06 – Hardtravelin' Fest (day 1): Flotilla Way, Allies, Fuckedupmess, Aydin
8/19/06 – Hardtravelin' Fest (day 2): the sea, like lead, Sinaloa, Life At These Speeds, He Taught Me Lies
8/22/06 – Terminal State, Build Your Weapons, Pyramid Scheme
8/24/06 – Snake Apartment, Shit Mayor, Thrak, Human Sick
8/25/06 – Agnosis, Village of Dead Roads, Come to Dust, Fantasy Boyfriend
8/30/06 – Strung Up, Direct Control, Caustic Christ, Brain Handle
9/2/06 – Pyramid Scheme, FLAK, Destroy the Orcs, Defend Means Attack
9/4/06 – Blank Stare, Positive Reinforcement, Warzone Womyn, Pyramid Scheme
9/8/06 – Big Idea benefit w/ Sequoia, the sea, like lead, Allies, Wormsmeat, Kahzmik Crystal Muff
9/12/06 – He Taught Me Lies, Defiance Ohio, Whiskey Smile
9/16/06 – Chronic Seizure, Wasted Time, Formaldehyde Junkies cover band, Brain Handle
9/18/06 – Kayo Dot
9/24/06 – Sunday Morning Einsteins, Brain Handle, FLAK, Blood Vessels to Wires
9/26/06 – Hudson Falcons, Maybe Pete, The War Is On
10/1/06 – By My Hands, Animal Mother, Full Collapse, Lacing Restraint, Leavenworth
10/6/06 – Allies, Blues Skies Collapse, Caspian, The Exit Strategy, Lemuria
10/12/06 – Aydin, Flotilla Way, Smells Like Gina
10/13/06 – Endless Mike and the Beagle Club, The Static Transistor, Wrestling Secrets, Man at Arms
10/19/06 – Perkins Family Restaurant, Mourning After, 86 Mentality, Cardiac Arrest

10/22/06 – Hulk Smash, Tunturi, Thrak, Bibulous Chap
10/23/06 – Hero Dishonest, Acts of Sedition, Warzone Womyn, Night Terror
10/27/06 – Wartorn, Choose Your Poison, Boom Boom Kid, Blood Vessels to Wires, Mourning After
10/30/06 – Immortal Avenger, Meltdown, Magic Wolf
11/5/06 – Kim Phuc, Brain Handle, Caustic Christ
11/10/06 – ADD IX: Sleep Little One Sleep, Build Your Weapons, Tusk Lord, Isha and Zetta, Flotilla Way, Pyramid Scheme, Fuck Telecorps, Meltdown, Thrak, Weird Paul
11/30/06 – Bathtub Shitter, Warzone Womyn, Tunturi, Tumor Feast
12/2/06 Weird Paul, The Rhodora, The Bumps, Styles For Modern Living
12/21/06 – Appalachian Terror Unit, Night Terror, Blood Vessels to Wires

2007

1/2/07 – Night Terror, Brain Handle, Social Circle
1/4/07 – Death Before Dishonor, Ignite The Wall, Shallow Water Grave, Another Breath, Path To Misery
1/6/07 – Seasick, ANS, Pyramid Scheme, Thrak
1/7/07 – The Silent Drive, FC Five, Hank Jones, The Tradition, Full Collapse
1/12/07 – Potboiler, Tin Armour, Lucas Sloppy's Flying Organ
1/13/07 – Baby Bird, Thrak, Mans, Warzone Womyn, Terminal Youth
1/16/07 – The Flash Attacks, Gabe Zander
1/18/07 – Tiny Hawks, Ultradolphins, Sleep Little One Sleep
1/19/07 – Cover Show: MITB/Neanderthal, Formaldahyde Junkies, Neil Young, 25 Ta Life, Minutemen, Nirvana
1/20/07 – Cover Show: Cro Mags, Born Against, Andrew WK, Beastie Boys, Black Sabbath
1/30/07 – A Dying Dream, It Prevails, Monument The Ghost, Full Collapse
2/2/07 – The Loved Ones, Zolof The Rock And Roll Destroyer, Kilowatt, Meanstreak
2/3/07 – Ghost Mice, The Max Levine Ensemble, Delay, Whiskey Smile, Boogdish
2/6/07 – The Never, Endless Mike and The Beagle Club, The Flash Darlings
2/7/07 – With Blood Comes Cleansing, Thumbscrew, ABACABB, Sealing The Gates, Failure To Fall
2/9/07 – The Feelers, Retainers, Caustic Christ, FLAK
2/10/07 – Man The Conveyors, Behind Enemy Lines, Mourning After, Night Terror
2/23/07 – "Harder They Fall: A Tribute to Integrity" release show w/ Know The Score, Crowd Deterrent, Unreal City, Under One Flag, The Come Up, Without Restraint
2/24/07 – Bane, Down To Nothing, Ambitions, The Geeks, Van Damage, The Statis Transistor
2/26/07 – Means, Those Who Fear, Calm The Storm, Horwood, Jaded Holly
2/28/07 – I Object, Tangled Lines
3/2/07 – These Green Eyes, Sullivan Avenue, Migrations, Cali AC
3/9/07 – Government Warning, Wasted Time, Brain Handle, Pyramid Scheme, Cross Laws
3/17/07 – Acid Reflux, Pyramid Scheme, Night Terror
3/22/07 – Hot Cross, He Taught Me Lies, Allies, Invention of Monsters
3/30/07 – Tierra De Nadie, Envenomed, Behind Enemy Lines, Mourning After
3/31/07 – Boring Girls, The War Is On, Face The Panic
4/4/07 – I Adapt, Die Young, Ultradolphins, Path To Misery, Brain Handle
4/10/07 – The Fad, Unarmed, The Innocent, Kiwi Punch
4/16//07 – The Vicious, Caustic Christ, Kim Phuc
4/19/07 – Hi Watt Hex, Brutal Knights, American Cheeseburger
4/21/07 – Tusk Lord, Juhyo, Antennacle, Bastard Noise
4/29/07 – Total Fury, The Jury, Reagan SS, Cheap Tragedies, Caustic Christ, Brain Handle
5/4/07 – Plastered Bastards, Blood Vessels To Wires, Thrak
5/5/07 – Punk Rock Flea Market followed by Pyramid Scheme (7" release), Babybird, Night Terror
5/8/07 – In Defence, Warzone Womyn, Icon Gallery, FLAK
5/15/07 – Brain Handle (record release), Midnite Snake, Thrak, Tusk Lord
5/18/07 – Iskra, The Communion, Blood Vessels To Wires
5/23/07 – Landmines, The Maxipads, Mean Streak, The Innocent
5/26/07 – Problems, He Taught Me Lies, Styles For Modern Living, Josephy
6/1/07 – Benefit for Andy Stepanian of the SHAC7 w/ screening of "Behind The Mask" and music by Path To Misery, He Taught Me Lies, Biocastle
6/2/07 – Outbreak, Wake Up Call!, Monument The Ghost, The War Is On, Bold at Heart
6/10/07 – Life Crisis, The War Is On, Blood Vessels to Wires, Thrak
6/22/07 – Joe Jack Talcum, Weird Paul Rock Band, Ukebox, Daddy
6/23/07 – Get Rad, FLAK, Night Terror
6/28/07 – Look Back and Laugh, Caustic Christ, Brain Handle, Forced March, Autistic Youth
6/29/07 – Wartorn, Choose Your Poison, Black September, Blood Vessels to Wires
6/30/07 – Des Ark, He Taught Me Lies, Julie Sokolow, Every Monster Truck Ever
7/2/07 – Die Yong, Ruiner, Unreal City, Incommunicado Lifespan
7/8/07 – SMD, Thrak, Beyond Thunderdome
7/9/07 – Ceremony, Allegiance, Pyramid Scheme, Unit 731
7/10/07 – California Love, Slices, Blood Vessels to Wires, Night Terror

7/12/07 – Crime In Stereo, Hank Jones, Attitude, At All Costs,The Static Transistor
7/13/07 – Bill+Rachel's Wedding Celebration w/ Thought Crime, Caustic Christ, Brain Handle, Night Terror
7/15/07 – Mind Eraser, Scapegoat, Thrak, Baby Bird
7/16/07 – Potboiler, Traffic and Weather, The Frantic Heart of It
7/18/07 – The Fad, The Waffle Stompers, Royal City Riot
7/21/07 – Think Fast, Pyramid Scheme, Thrak
7/23/07 – Dustheads, FLAK, Night Terror
7/24/07 – Terror Level Red, Oh Shit They're Going To Kill Us, Blood Vessels to Wires, Leprosy 76
7/25/07 – Yo Man Go!, Bridge and Tunnel, Ringers, Flotilla Way, Icon Gallery
7/26/07 – Daggermouth, Flash Darlings, Full Collapse, Die Rote Kapelle
7/28/07 – Warzone Womyn, Conversions, Conquest for Death, Breakfast
7/31/07 – Under Pressure, Dry-rot, Unreal City, Pyramid Scheme
8/15/07 – Have Heart, Death Before Dishonor, Rise and Fall, Meltdown, Draught
8/16/07 – Know The Score, Fight Like Hell
8/19/07 – Weekend Nachos, Thrak
8/20/07 – Witch Hunt, Margaret Thrasher, Plastered Bastards, Icon Gallery
8/21/07 – Sweat Lodge, Hulk Out, Fuck Telecorps, Night Terror
8/25/07 – Benefit for 'Building New Hope' w/ He Taught Me Lies, Rick Gribenas, Aydin, Allies
8/28/07 – Be My Doppelganger, The Shuttlecocks, Johnny and the Razorblades
8/30/07 – Harley Poe, Channel Scorpion News, Die Rote Kapelle, Saber-teeth, Coming Through The Rye
9/5/07 – Ghost Mice, Ned:, The Gadabout Film Festival, Northern Aggression
9/7/07 – Casket Architects, Sariacc, Die Rote Kapelle, Shrike Beats Bee, Dinosores, Drought
9/11/07 – Rotten Cadaver, Slices, Abysme
9/14/07 – Cover Show: Punk Mixtape, Pissed Jeans, Cyndi Lauper, Queers, Screeching Weasel
9/15/07 – Cover Show: Deep Purple, Weakerthans, Dillinger Four, Billy Bragg, Suicide
9/19/07 – Double Negative, Caustic Christ, Night Terror
9/21/07 – Civic Progress, Slices, Mike Siciliano
9/27/07 – Baroness, Black Tusk, Icon Gallery
10/7/07 – Creepout, Swear To God, Crowd Deterrent, American Werewolves
10/14/07 – Modern Life Is War, Trash Talk, Trap Them, I Adapt
10/16/07 – Death Before Dishonor, Damnation AD, Unholy, Unit 731, Drought
10/18/07 – Two If By Sea, Kiwi Punch, Dan Dabber, The Fad
10/20/07 – Nancy, Bridgely Moore, The Shuttlecocks
10/27/07 – FLAK (record release), Night Terror, Kim Phuc
10/30/07 – Endless Mike and the Beagle Club, Lemuria, Everything, Now!, Everthus the Deadbeats, Book of Pridemore
11/7/07 – Slingshot Dakota, Flotilla Way, Branches!
11/9/07 – ADD Fest X
11/14/07 – Uptight, Horseback, Kahoutek, Mike Tamburo
11/15/07 – Call It Arson, Wrench In The Works, Flash Darlings, Overseas, Drought, Lung Rip
11/17/07 – Bear Is Driving, Hulk Smash, DBL Dish
11/19/07 – Rat City Riot, The War Is On, Do Crimes, Empty Handed
11/20/07 – Orgone (CD release), Architect, Full Collapse, The County
11/24/07 – The Degenerics, Fanshen, FLAK, Pyramid Scheme
11/26/07 – The Rebel Spell
11/30/07 – Midnight, Villians, Abysme, Oh Shit They're Going To Kill Us
12/1/07 – Unreal City, Steel Nation, Trapped Under Ice, Where It Ends, Pulling Teeth
12/6/07 – Soft Sickle, Slices, Thrak, Iron Lung, Hatred Surge
12/10/07 – Pulling Teeth, Where It Ends, Trapped Under Ice, Steel Nation, Unreal City
12/21/07 – Terror, Unreal City, Sacred Pledge, Unit 731

2008

1/1/08 – Zegota, Born Bad, Slices, Auryn
1/3/08 – Unholy, Wrathcobra, Path to Misery, Stinkpalm Death
1/5/08 – In Defence, Juice Tyme, Pyramid Scheme, Thrak
1/6/08 – Static Radio, Seasick, Static Transistor, Drought
1/8/08 – Cheap Time, Wax Museums, Brain Handle, Burndowns
1/10/08 – Screaming Females, Dirty Faces, The Library is on Fire
1/17/08 – FPO, Attake, Auryn
1/19/200 – Paralyzer, Thrak, Soft Sickle, Reptile
1/25/08 – Kiwi Punch, The Fad, Atilla and the Huns, The Hormones
2/2/08 – LaGrecia, Incommunicado, Northern Aggression
2/4/08 – Reign Supreme, Meltdown, Deathright, Turnpike Gates
2/5/08 – Jookabox, Doog, Grybus, Pikock
2/29/08 – Neptune, Meatweaver, Full Color
3/1/08 – Black Dove, Brain Handle, Night Terror
3/6/08 – After the Bombs, FLAK, Night Terror, Wrath Cobra
3/7/08 – Slices, In The Belly of the Whale, Cock Scene Investigators
3/8/08 – Blues Control, Sun Tornado, Mike Tamburo & Josh Beyer, Altaic
3/9/08 – Trap Them, Path to Misery, Bearathon, Kim Phuc
3/17/08 – SFN, Pyramid Scheme, Thrak, Slices
3/22/08 – Tropiezo, Golpe Justo, La Armada, No Slogan, Unreal City

3/26/08 – Sunpower, Redfox, Not Today
3/29/08 – Classic Dischord Covers Night to Benefit Roboto: bands covering Shudder to Think, Ignition, Scream, Minor Threat, Rites of Spring, Gray Matter
3/31/08 Tugnut, Kamikabe, Shrike Beats Bee, Sarlacc
4/12/08 – Forca Macabra, Kuolema, Icon Gallery, Do Crimes
4/14/08 – From the Depths, Path to Misery, Drugdealer, Auryn
4/16/08 – Giant, Khann, Bearathon
4/19/08 – Disfear, Parasytic, Unreal City, Abysme, Saint Jude
4/20/08 – Casket Architects, Church of Snake, Pikock, Sarlacc, Shirke Beats Bee
4/25/08 – Ol' Scratch, Admiral Browning, Hodag Redux Delux, Teeth
4/26/08 – Slices, Do Crimes, Not Today, Girlfight
4/27/08 – Paint It Black, Cloak/Dagger, Kim Phuc, The Static Transistor
5/3/08 – Daylight Robbery, The Fitt, Soft Sickle
5/7/08 – Blacklisted, Not Today, Deathright, Turnpike Gates
5/9/08 – Pulling Teeth, Gray Ghost, Bad Habit, Pyramid Scheme Deathright
5/10/08 – Under Pressure, Slices, Not Today, Glued Up and Speeding
5/19/08 – Mutators, Modern Creatures, Maxi-Pads
5/22/08 – Coffins, The Endless Blockade, Hellnation, Slices, Abysme
5/23/08 – Invasion, Chronic Seizure, Kim Phuc, Do Crimes
5/30/08 – Black Dove, Gasmask Terror, Protestant, Auryn, Drought
6/2/08 – Seasick, Zhenia Golov, The Static Transistor, Not Today
6/5/08 – Cheap Girls, Halo Fauna, Full Color
6/6/08 – Brody's Militia, Plastered Bastards, Long to Hell
6/7/08 – Condominium, Brain Handle, Good Luck
6/13/08 – American Cheeseburger, Brain Handle, Thrak, Pig God and Goat Crown
6/15/08 – Last Chance to Reason, Hero Destroyed, Drugdealer, Salo
6/16/08 – Red Dons, Estranged, Kim Phuc, Icon Gallery
6/17/08 – Against Empire, Wrathcobra, Do Crimes
6/18/08 – No Turning Back, I Rise, Wake Up Call, Drought
6/19/08 – Nice People, Mountain Asleep, Algernon Cadwallader, Bowhunter
6/24/08 – Backstabbers Inc, Wasteland, Drought, Soft Sickle
6/26/08 – Consular, Token Black Guy, Bastard, Implant Grade
6/27/08 – Stout
6/29/08 – Life Trap, Citizens Patrol, Brain Handle, Not Today
7/3/08 – Lewd Acts, Flase Positive, Pyramid Scheme, Drought
7/6/08 – Punch, Not Today, Dead Bodies for Sheilds
7/17/08 – Slingshot Dakota, Branches, Aydin
7/18/08 – FNB Benefit
7/19/08 – The State, Caustic Christ, Auryn, Absurd System
7/24/08 – ANS, Reproach, From the Depths, Masochrist,
7/25/08 – Path to Misery
7/27/08 – They & The Children, Pyramid Scheme, Dead Uncles
8/1/08 – Guida, Black September, Abysme
8/5/08 – The Static Transistor, The Riot Before, Endless Mike and The Beagle Club, Red Team Blue Team
8/10/08 – Nice View, Hellnation, Caustic Christ, Abysme, This Time Tomorrow
8/11/08 – Screaming Females, Full Color, Allies
8/16/08 – Half Gorilla, Masochrist, Mammoth Bath
8/20/08 – Pyramid Scheme, Glued Up and Speeding
9/4/08 – Featherlight
9/5/08 – Bought in Blood
9/16/08 – My Epic
9/20/08 – Punx Picnic
9/28/08 – Dean Dirg, The Young, Brain Handle, Pyramid Scheme
9/29/08 – Cop on Fire, Behind Enemy Lines, Plastered Bastards
10/4/08 – Lewd Acts, Intense Ovens of Fred
10/9/08 – Cola Freaks, Slices, Glued Up and Speeding
10/11/08 – Creep Out, Crowd Deterrent, Numb, Unreal City, Coffin Bros
10/20/08 – An Albatross, Frank n' Gary, Microwaves, Drugdealer
10/21/08 – Acts of Sedition
10/22/08 – Stolen Minks
10/24/08 – Girlfight, The Last Hope, Circus Circus, Failure to Fall, Nancy Drew
10/25/08 – Dark Castle, Deathbeds, Salo, RJ Myato
10/31/08 – Parasytic
11/1/08 – Code Orange Kids
11/7/08 – Gutwrench
11/8/08 – ADD Fest XI: Drought, Masochrist, Onodrim, Red Fox, Savage Lines, Glued Up and Speeding, Castle, Pikock, Bowhunter, Long to Hell
11/9/08 – This is Hell, Terminate, Eyes Wide Shut
11/13/08 – Have Heart, Blacklisted, Ceremony, Convicted, Letdown
11/14/08 – Mind of Asian, Sonorous Gale, Long to Hell, Unwelcome Guests
11/16/08 – Rosetta
11/17/08 – Walls, Brain Handle, Kim Phuc, Slices
11/18/08 – Guided Cradle, Behind Enemy Lines, Dishonor, Auryn
11/19/08 – Off With Their Heads, American Armada, Red Team/Blue Team, The Hormones
11/28/08 – Annihilation Time, Do Crimes, Plastered Bastards, Subway Blastrag
12/6/08 – Blood & Cupcakes Blood Drive
12/17/08 – Who Goes There, Loose Lips Sink Ships, Masochrist, In the Wake of Giants
12/20/08 – DIY KaijuFest: Art Show (Jeff Lamm, Velocitron, Beak, Hauntkraft)

2009

1/4/09 – Bubonic Bear, The Last Hope, Girlfight, Drought, Wrestling Secrets
1/13/09 – Seasick, Killin' It, Soft Sickle, Confidence Men
1/21/09 – Beartrap, Mammoth Bath, Bear Skull, Unreal City, Disfigurement
1/26/09 – The Abominable Iron Sloth, Blownupnihilist, Drugdealer
2/7/09 – Stations, Lost Cause, Icon Gallery
2/19/09 – Bosque, Expendable Youth, Confidence Men
2/21/09 – The Adalusians, Allies, Soft Sickle
2/25/09 – Cruel Hand, Hank Jones, His Day Has Come, Terminate
2/26/09 – Snowstorm, Onodrim, Johnmarkarr
2/2709 – Remeber Thy Name, The Fail Safe, Maesion, Girlfight
3/6/09 – Sick Fix, Coke Bust, Slices
3/10/09 – Comedy Show: Greg Barris, John Wells, Jermaine Fowler
3/12/09 – Divisions, Do Crimes, Confidence Men, Virgin Birth
3/14/09 – Deathright, Widower, Smoke and Mirrors, Bowhunter, Bad Moons, Monument The Ghost
3/15/09 – Deep Sleep, Psyched to Die, Dought, Masochrist
3/16/09 – Masshysteri, Kim Phuc, Confidence Men
3/20/09 – Kingdom, From Hell, Abaddon, Failure to Fall
3/26/09 – Fall of Efrafa, Protestant, Onodrim, Auryn
3/27/09 – Helsinki, Resin Hits, South Carey, Ukiah
3/28/09 – Motorpsychos, Plastered Bastards, Divine Tragedy
3/29/09 – La Crisi, Strength Approach, Hank Jones, The Steel Nation
3/30/09 – Nuclear Family, Icon Gallery, Confidence Men
4/8/09 – Condenada, Icon Gallery
4/12/09 – Landmine Marathon, Microwaves, Mamoth Bath, Complete Failure
4/18/09 – Part of Totally Wired Fest: Brain Handle, Manikins, The Yolks, Smith Westerns, Slices, Plates, Flying Tchreros, Naw Dude
4/27/09 – Braveyoung, Arms, Edhochuli
4/28/09 – 108, Soul Control, I Rise, Complete Failure, Soft Sickle
4/29/09 – Hjertestop, Brain Handle, Virgin Birth
5/9/09 – Egality, Deathright, Disfigurement, Masochrist
5/13/09 – He Taught Me Lies, Onodrim, Hidden Twin, Full Color
5/19/09 – The Effort, Failure To Fall, Eyes Wide Shut, Terminate
5/25/09 – Unreal City, Kim Phuc, Slices
5/27/09 – Plauge, Shards, Do Crimes, Confience Men
5/28/09 – Vile Intent, Thrak, Masochrist
5/29/09 – Vile Gash, Nordic Waste, The Understanables, Slices, Virgin Birth, Punkmen and the Chump
5/31/09 – Rosetta, Arms, Ancient Shores, Girlfight
6/1/09 – Suburban Showdown, Plastered Bastards, Dishonor
6/12/09 – Salo, Black Block, Brain Pollution, Ascites
6/18/09 – Chronic Seizure, Confidence Men, Mammoth Bath
6/24/09 – Loser Life, Soft Sickle, Confidence Men
6/25/09 – Cult Ritual, Vile Gash, Slices, Virgin Birth
6/30/09 – Trophy Wife, The Curtains of Night, Drugdealer
7/3/09 – Failure To Fall, Wreak Havoc, MTG, Deathright, Belie My Burial
7/5/09 – Fucked for Life, Cognitive Dissonance, Auryn, Short Dark Strangers, Do Crimes
7/12/09 – Also Lasers, The Ginger Envelope, Madeline
7/16/09 – Brain Killer, P.S. Eliot, Hop Along Queen Ansleis, Slices, Secret Tombs
7/20/09 – Force Fed
7/21/09 – Hatred Surge, Mammoth Grinder, Punch, Heartless, Masochrist
7/27/09 – Benefit for G-20 Resistance w/ From the Depths, The Seperation, Orphans, Froeseph
7/23/09 – Orphans, The Only Threat, Code Orange Kids, G.O.S., The Edukators
8/4/09 – Drought, Heartless, Masakari, Swallowed Up, Cursed Knife
8/6/09 – Intifada, The Men, Masochrist, Confidence Men, A fight with Sledgehammers
8/7/09 – Landlord, Witches, Secret Tombs
8/14/09 – Bitter End, Do Crimes, Daily Void, Zhenia Golov Confidence Men, Virgin Birth
8/16/09 – Black Dove, Preying Hands Assymetric Warfare, Auryn, Masochrist
8/17/09 – Gun Outfit, Plainswalkers, Secret Tombs, Punkmen,
8/19/09 – The Static Transistor, Asinine, Sidekicks, Code Orange Kids
8/21/09 – Alpha & Omega, OVERMARS, Battlefields
8/24/09 – Crime in Stereo, Failure to Fall, His Day Has Come
8/27/09 – Heath Deadger, Isolation, Drought, Old Accusers
9/9/09 – Regrets, Peregrine, Heartless, Broken Neck
9/19/09 – Kakistocracy, Peregrine, Virgin Birth
10/11/09 – Girlfight, Consumer, Ancient Shores, Who Goes There? Seas We Fail to Sail
10/18/09 – I Decide, Thrak, Masochrist, Broken Neck
10/22/09 – Nothing To Nothing, Dead Icons, Failure to Fall, Old Accusers, STS
10/31/09 – Death Before Dishonor, Forfeit, Steel Nation, Unit 731
11/13/09 – ADD FEST XII and Roboto's 10th Bday: Cottonball Man, Virgin Birth, Secret Tombs, Ragweed Season, Dire Wolves, Tay-Sach, Heartless, Forest Dweller, Code Orange Kids, Coal Miner
12/4/09 – Onodrim, Birds and Wires, Blood Red
12/5/09 – Brace War, Backtrack, Heartless, Old Accusers
12/15/09 – Caulfield, Dead Heroes, Broken Neck, Cursed Knife, Drought

12/19/09 – Path to Misery, Peregrine, As this Body I Exist, Failure to Fall, Torch Runner, Systems

12/26/09 – Lemuria, Unreal City, Heartless, Thrak, Masochrist, Old Accusers

2010

1/14/10 – Brain Killer, Scapegoat, Slices, General Interest

1/22/10 – Pianos Become Teeth, In the Hollows, Girlfight

1/31/10 – Through this Defiance, The War is On, Vow of Hatred, Enemy Mind

2/3/10 – Confidence Men, Secret Tombs, The Sorely Trying Days, Code Orange Kids

2/18/10 – Shai Hulud, Path To Misery

2/20/10 – Consumer, Broken Neck, Masochrist, Confidence, Code Orange Kids

2/22/10 – Tiger Flowers, March of Echoes, Peregrine

2/25/10 – Nothing to Nothing, Broken Neck, Failure to Fall

2/26/10 – Brain Handle, Slices, Hidden Twin, Ice Capades, Weird Paul

2/27/10 – Secret Tombs, Allies, HTML (2pm Show, Art Raffle, and Record Swap)

2/27/10 – The Endless Blockade, Warzone Womyn, XBrainiaX, Paralyzer

2/28/10 – Braveyoung, Broken Neck, No Time For Love, Dead Horse

* We pieced this list together as best we could. If you have any additional information about shows or corrections to the list, please get in touch by sending an email to robotobook@gmail.com.

Acknowledgements

The editors thank the following people and entities for their help in creating this book; without them, it wouldn't exist: Mac Howison and everyone at the Sprout Fund, Emma Rehm and Jen Briselli for transcription and general assistance, Alyssa Truszkowski and Cindy Yogmas for their input, Steel City Media, and of course, the Mr. Roboto Project.

We would specifically like to thank the following photographers for use of their photographs: Shawn Brackbill, Sarah Carr, Tanner Douglass, Charissa Hamilton-Gribenas, John Herrington, Deanna Hitchcock, Chris Boarts Larson, Chistopher Schwarzott and Brad Quartuccio.

Thanks to Mike Budai for the cover art.

Thanks to t.he Mr. Roboto Project and the many other individuals who let us borrow their flyers, posters and other documents.

Thanks to everyone who agreed to be interviewed for this book and those who submitted anecdotes for inclusion.

Thanks to Alyssa Truszkowski and Christopher James for use of their video footage.

Thanks to all the bands who donated their music for inclusion on the DVD.

Special thanks to the following individuals who served on the Roboto Board of Directors during its 10+ years in Wilkinsburg:

Mike Q. Roth
Deanna Hitchcock
Doug Mosurock
Justin Cummings
Ian Ryan
Jessica Ghilani
Dave Romano
Eileen Nall
Eric Meisberger

Jeremy Hedges
Jeremy Carson
David Huggins-Daines
Jen Briselli
Joseph Wilk
Michael Siciliano
Jim Robinson
Mike Ovens
Mike Bolam

Brian Gruetze
Greg Mantooth
xAJx
Kyle Folsom
Tim Robes
Jessie Buckner
Jeff Gentle
Alyssa Truszkowski

DVD contents

The DVD enclosed with this book includes a collection of 37 songs by Pittsburgh bands that either helped define the Mr. Roboto Project or were themselves highly defined by Roboto. Most of these bands no longer exist. We've noted below which bands are still active as of the printing of this book. Many of these bands do have other recordings still available. We encourage you to track them down.

Pikadori / Anthem
Choke City / Track one
Counteraction / Sadly Beautiful
Crucial Unit / Thrashaholics Unanimous
Behind Enemy Lines / Devastated
Disturbed Youth / Punched in the Face
Fate of Icarus / The Shepherd's Tools
Caustic Christ / Burned
Fear is the Mindkiller / The Third Road
Modey Lemon (active) / Caligula
Alpha Control Group C / Good Furniture
Microwaves (active) / XXY
Creation is Crucifixion / Preditor/Prey
Free Barrabas / Conditioned and Corrupted
Gunspiking / Move
Grand Buffet (active) / You're On Fire
Teddy Duchamp's Army / New Moog
Io / Reigned
McCarthy Commission / Battered and Bruised

Whatever It Takes / Green Light, Yellow Light, Stop
Mary Celeste / Departures
Aphasia / Keep Your Legs Closed and Your Cock in Your Pants
Conelrad / The Pincher
He Taught Me Lies / Stonewall
Intense Youth / Tradition
Ice Capades / 15-1
Sequoia / Bird Fight
Krooked Grind / But It Still Moves
the sea, like lead / So Say We All
Vale and Year / Singletary
Stilyagi / The Orbit
Suburban Death Machine / Filled Up
Thrak / Slime of Power
Kim Phuc (active) / Wormwood Star
Pyramid Scheme / Less is More
Warzone Womyn / Cobblestone Stomach
Brain Handle / Sound of a Frightened Man

In addition, the DVD contains video of some of these bands performing at the first Roboto space. It also has a digital and searchable version of the Roboto show list, and extra images, including show fliers.

To use the DVD, stick it in a computer and open the file named "OpenMeFirst." (This is a data DVD, and won't work in a DVD player. You'll need a web browser and a DVD-capable drive.)